Law & Economics

Property, Contracts, Torts

Demetri Kantarelis

Business correspondence should be addressed to the publisher:

Business & Economics Society International (B&ESI)
64 Holden Street
Worcester, MA 01605-3109
USA
Tel: (508) 852-3937
Fax: (508) 595-0089
Email: hkan@besiweb.com, Web Site: http://www.besiweb.com

ISBN-10: 0-9659831-8-8
ISBN-13: 978-0-9659831-8-1

Printed, on acid-free paper, in the United States of America

To my Family,

for letting me experience the kind of love

that people, without hesitation, die for.

Acknowledgements

I am grateful to my students at Assumption College for inspiration and, most importantly, their unlimited patience as readers of several drafts prior to completion.

For critical and constructive comments, suggestions, corrections and direction I am indebted to the anonymous reviewers of the various journals (see Preface – End Notes) that originally published the papers containing most of the ideas presented here.

For the many discussion sessions and for reading various sections, I would like to thank Jörg Borrmann (University of Vienna, Austria), Richard Freije (Sun Life, USA) and my colleagues at Assumption College, Thomas White, Dylan McGee and Stuart Lynn. I have also benefited from discussions with Morris Altman (University of Newcastle, Australia) and Nathan Berg (University of Otago, New Zealand).

Finally, I would like to thank the publisher for editorial, marketing and technical support.

Brief Biography

Demetri Kantarelis is Professor of Economics at Assumption College (USA) where he teaches in both the undergraduate and MBA programs. His research focuses, primarily, on industrial organization as well as law and economics themes and has appeared in the *Quarterly Journal of Business and Economics, Journal of Socio-Economics, Journal of Economic Behavior and Organization, International Journal of Law & Management, Contemporary Readings in Law and Social Justice, International Journal of Business Continuity & Risk Management, International Journal of Management Concepts and Philosophy* and several others. He has authored *Theories of the Firm 4th ed*, co-authored *Essentials of Inferential Statistics* 5th ed and co-founded the Interdisciplinary Environmental Association. He currently serves as editor of the *International Journal of Economics & Business Research* and the *Interdisciplinary Environmental Review* as well as on the editorial or advisory boards of several other academic journals.

Demetri Kantarelis, Ph.D.
Professor of Economics
Department of Economics & Global Studies
Assumption College, 500 Salisbury Street
Worcester, MA 01609-1296, USA

Contents

Preface

My hope is that this textbook would serve, as a supplement, intermediate level economics and pre-law or law school students in their educational endeavors. By relying on microeconomics, I try to describe important theorems, models and applications associated with property, contracts, and torts.[1]

More specifically, in Chapter 1 (titled ***Property Rights***)[2], I review the Coasean underpinnings of basic property law as it relates to externalities and pollution permits. Additionally, I make an attempt to broaden the Coase invariance theorem by including asymmetry of information. Given the probability distributions of strong and weak types of property-disputing parties, I show how incentive-compatible legal rules may be constructed to eliminate some problems associated with information asymmetry. The modified theorem I propose may be stated as follows: when transaction costs (such as search costs, bargaining costs and enforcement costs) are zero, incentive-compatible deals, mediated by the legal system, give rise to efficient allocation of resources, irrespective of the legal assignment of property rights. Moreover, I discuss possible negatives associated with property taxes and the lack of secure property titles in developing nations.

In Chapter 2 (titled ***Contracts***)[3], I rely on simple mathematics, graphs and verbal arguments to describe concepts (such as adverse selection and moral hazard) in an attempt to offer a justification as to why the profit-making firm may be viewed as a function of its nucleus expertise and a risky portfolio of contracts. I attempt to demonstrate, theoretically, that a profit-making entity can experience higher profit if it reduces, thorough diversification, the risk of its portfolio of promisor-type and promisee-type deals. In its effort to reduce such risk, the firm needs to know each deal's profit share and be able to estimate each dealing partner's reliability (a random variable). I point out that the more a firm considers factors such as mediation, optimal commitments, and the like, the more effective and efficient becomes the management of a portfolio of deals. As explained through examples and illustrations, viewing the firm as a function of deals may be of value to today's global, knowledge-based, outsourcing / insourcing firms which may find it increasingly difficult to rely on conventional contracts. I point out that efficient and effective deals benefit the co-signing entities as well as other stakeholders (community, region, nation, etc.); e.g., deals contribute to competitiveness (by reducing costs or improving productivity or both) and as a result to more profit, income and growth.

In Chapter 3 (titled ***Contracts & Banking***)[4], I describe a conventional, representative, model about an integrated firm, which simultaneously sells assets and lends money to asset buyers (homogeneous or heterogeneous in terms of risk-type), and discuss various theoretical principles (primarily lessons on how to minimize adverse selection and moral hazard in lending.) In turn, I make an attempt to contrast the model's principles against the great recession especially as it relates to sub-prime lending in the USA and I conclude that the model's theoretical principles were violated due to lack of well-thought out contracts. It is stated that the unusually large international capital inflows into US capital markets, the easy monetary policy, the harmful practice of "originate-to-distribute" loans along with securitization based on faulty ratings, and the anti-regulation efforts of past governments to promote financial capital democratization, blocked lenders' efforts (took away incentives) to minimize adverse selection and moral hazard, caused the real-estate bubble and triggered the 2007-08 financial global crisis.

In Chapter 4 (titled ***Torts***)[5], I make an attempt to help law and economics students to better understand the implications of marginal precautionary costs and marginal expected harms in the process of cost internalization. By relying on the concepts of liability, negligence, precaution and various methodologies for the estimation of compensatory damages, I discuss incentive mechanisms and procedures for cost internalization by both potential defendants and plaintiffs.

In Chapter 5 (titled ***Occupational Stress: Potential for Tort Litigation***)[6], I attempt to capture the essence of issues associated with occupational stress by relying on microeconomic theoretical as well as popular and professional press summaries that appear to justify the underlying logic of the points made. Firstly, assuming that stress is a factor of production and that a firm functions in an environment free of any regulation, I propose a model which predicts that the profit maximizing stress level (S*) is less than the stress level that maximizes output. Secondly, I point out that reduction below S* may be achieved only if a firm's increase in cost for stress relief in the work place guarantees productivity and profit improvement in exchange for a reduction in employee health damages/costs due to stress. Thirdly, assuming that a stress standard inside the firm can be identified, compliance with that standard by reallocating stress from one group of employees to another or from one production plant to another may contribute to a reduction in total damages to employees and/or to a reduction in total stress relief expenditures to the firm. Fourthly, a regulated firm subject to a standard, decided upon outside the firm, may trigger unintended outcomes due to miss-estimation of that standard: if the standard is considerably less than S*, the firm may not have the incentive to comply. It is emphasized that beyond a certain point, stress and its measurement in the work place becomes very difficult to handle due to conditions in personal life and information asymmetries: (a) How much of the observed stress is due to work or personal life and how interdependent are the two? (b) How should a firm minimize problems associated with asymmetries in occupational stress information that may lead to hold up, adverse selection and moral hazard? [2]

Endnotes

1. Endnotes are stated and references are reported at the end of each chapter.

2. Material in this chapter is reprinted from Anderson Emily & Demetri Kantarelis; "Incentive-Compatibility and Coasean Invariance in Property Affairs", *Contemporary Readings in Law and Social Justice*, Volume 8(2), 2016, pp. 96114, with permission from the Publisher (Addleton Academic Publishers.)

3. Material in this chapter is reprinted from Kantarelis, Demetri; The Firm as a Function of Deals, *International Journal of Law and Management*, 2014, Volume 56, Issue 4, pp.311-332, with permission from the Publisher (Emerald Group Publishing.)

4. Material in this chapter is reprinted from Kantarelis, Demetri; The Banking Firm: Theoretical Principles and their Violations in the USA, *International Journal of Business Continuity & Risk Management*, 2010, Volume 1, Issue 3, pp 222-232, with permission from the Publisher (Inderscience Publishers.)

5. Material in this chapter is reprinted from Kantarelis, Demetri; Internalization of Costs, Liability and Negligence, Performance and Reliance", *International Journal of Law & Management*,

2008, Volume 50, Issue 6, pp 274-284, with permission from the Publisher (Emerald Group Publishing.)

6. Material in this chapter is reprinted from Kantarelis, Demetri; Occupational Stress: Some Microeconomic Issues, *International Journal of Management Concepts and Philosophy*, 2005, Volume 1, #3, pp 232-247, with permission from the Publisher (Inderscience Publishers.)

Chapter 1:

Property Rights

I. Introduction

Legal rules about bundles of rights (or property law) are answers to questions such as those raised by Cooter and Ulen (p.71): "How are ownership rights established? What can be privately owned? What may owners do with their property? What are the remedies for the violation of property rights?" Answers (legal rules) are drafted subject to, primarily, various philosophical constraints as well as security and economic pragmatism.

Property law is influenced by philosophical views. According to the liberal philosopher John Rawls, as explained by Sen (p.12), we ought to desire to establish "specific institutions, firmly chosen for the basic structure of society (which) would demand one specific resolution of the principles of justice" but he does not explain "the difficulties in arriving at a unique set of principles to guide institutional choice". Sen questions this Rawlsian notion of "transcendental institutionalism" and he doubts that it is either possible or essential; in turn, he states that there is simply a plurality of philosophical principles (not only Rawls's liberal principles) that justify conflicting property claims.[1] As stated by Cooter and Ulen (pp.107-110), property has the capability to advance, among other, utilitarianism, justice, liberty and self-expression. More specifically,

On *utilitarian grounds,* it can be taken from (a person) in principle if the beneficiaries of the expropriation gain more in utility than the owner loses.

On *distributive justice grounds,* in Aristotle's conception, aristocrats use (wealth) for more worthy ends than do others. (Therefore), redistribution of property would favor the rich and penalize the poor. … Another school of philosophical thought … emphasizes a just process for defining and enforcing property rights rather than a just outcome.

On *liberty grounds,* private property has … been viewed by some philosophers as a bulwark against the dictatorial authority of governments … The U.S. Constitution was probably drafted with this idea in mind.

On *self-expression grounds,* the artist transforms natural objects and makes them the artist's own. … Creators' rights of ownership … (extend) beyond art to most of the works of humans.

On *natural selection grounds,* Eswaran and Neary (2014, p.206), demonstrate that, given evolutionarily stable preferences, "*producers value the output more than interlopers do*. In this way, natural selection hardwires attachment to the fruits of one's own labor more than attachment to the fruits of someone else's labor. The asymmetry in valuation arises because of the asymmetric role of the contesting individuals in production of the output. Asymmetric valuation generates an innate enforcement mechanism whereby a producer would spend more effort in defense of his output than would an interloper in its attempted appropriation." As the same authors state (p.221), their setting "provides an evolutionary basis for both the doctrine of first possession and Locke's labor theory of property rights, which are crucial ingredients of the philosophical and legal approaches to property rights."

Property law violations (dubbed negative externalities) are present whenever the well-being of consumers or the production possibilities of firms are negatively affected by the actions of other agents in society. Negative externalities give rise to market failure (which may be corrected through the imposition of standards, taxation and bargaining between the parties involved) and they may range from, among other, bilateral to multilateral and from intellectual to pollution (e.g, environmental, noise, and aesthetic) or from positional to those that involve informational asymmetry. Several specific case examples are instructive.

The often-cited case of *Pierson v. Post, 2 Am. Dec. 264 (N.Y. 1805)* illustrates an archetypal bilateral dispute. There, the Supreme Court of New York resolved that in order to own an animal, you must physically possess it. The facts of the case are simple: Post and his dogs hunted and pursued a fox along a beach. Pierson was cognizant of the hunt and stepped in just as Post would have succeeded in the chase, ultimately killing and claiming the dead fox for himself. Post argued that his property interest in the fox vested by virtue of the chase itself, thus Pierson violated his property rights by interfering and claiming the fox. The lower court agreed with Post, but on appeal Pierson prevailed. The Court held that while Pierson may have been impolite, he did not violate Post's property rights. The Court went on to explain that one can only own an animal he physically possesses, but an exception may apply when one has mortally wounded the animal and has not given up pursuit. The continued pursuit of an injured animal would, in essence, activate a property right because it shows an unequivocal intention to possess the animal, having already taken some ownership or possessive interest in it through the initial wounding and continued pursuit of the animal. While it may seem unfair to punish Post, despite his efforts, the court reasoned that a bright-line rule preserves peace and order in society. The dissent, however, challenged this notion, asserting that if the hunter is within reach or has a reasonable chance of taking the animal, as was Post, then it should be his. However, the majority was indeed persuaded not just by fairness but also by efficiency. To find that Post had a decisive property interest in the fox by merely chasing it, an intention that could be abandoned at any moment, would cause a flood of litigation.

Conversely in *Boomer v. Atlantic Cement Co.*, property rights proved to be more malleable than the court's hard-lined approach in *Pierson v. Post.* This case is an example of a more complex multilateral pollution case and is also instructive. Boomer and his neighbors filed suit against Atlantic Cement Company because dirt, smoke, and vibrations spewed from the factory. He argued that this was a private nuisance, as it interfered with the use and enjoyment of his nearby home. The trial court found in favor of Boomer, awarding temporary damages, though the court noted that it is the responsibility of the government to regulate pollution, not the courts. Boomer appealed to get an injunction, but the Appellate Court upheld the trial court decision. Boomer appealed again, still in pursuit of an injunction. The New York Supreme Court partially reversed the lower court's decision, granting permanent damages to Boomer, but not an injunction. The court reasoned that an injunction would be inappropriate because although Boomer undeniably suffered some damage from the operation of the factory, his damages were relatively small compared to the overall societal benefit of Atlantic's continued operation.

This notion of societal value weighed against, and often in favor of, the property interests of private individuals is an important concept as it suggests that though property rights may seem well-articulated by bright-lined rules, there are some circumstances where one's property rights are not so clear and are, in fact, uncertain. Specifically, in *Ploof v. Putnam,* 81 Vt. 471 (1908), Ploof and his family were forced to moor their boat at Putnam's dock on Lake Champlain as a severe storm suddenly approached. Putnam's servant untied Ploof's boat, which resulted in injury to Ploof and his family, as well as damage to the boat. Ploof alleged two counts against Putnam, first that he trespassed against Ploof when his servant negligently released his boat into the storm, and second, that Putnam's servant negligently unmoored the boat. As a general rule, the doctrine of necessity is especially significant in cases where human life is at risk. While the jury demurred both claims, on appeal the Supreme Court of Vermont determined that Putnam's servant acted within the scope of employment and Ploof did, in fact, moor his boat out of necessity to save human life and limb. While normally the law of trespass is fairly cut and dry, such that the use of another's property without permission would violate another's property right, this rule is supple where another's interest in the same property outweighs that of another.

Alternatively, in *Vincent v. Lake Erie Transportation Co.*, 124 N.W. 221 (Minn. 1910), a vessel owned by Lake Erie Transportation was moored at Vincent's dock. A storm ensued, causing $500 in damage to the dock. Vincent subsequently sued to recover the damage, alleging that the defendant had trespassed, and a jury found in his favor. Lake Erie Transportation appealed, arguing that it was not liable as its use of the dock was a private necessity. On appeal, the court ruled in favor of Vincent and opined that the defendant could not be liable for trespass, as private necessity is a valid defense. However, the vessel was secured to the dock in order to preserve the vessel, at the expense of the dock. Thus, though the defendant had acted under private necessity, which warranted his temporary use of Vincent's property, the resulting damage was recoverable.

Regarding intellectual property disputes, Hall, Helmers, Rogers, and Sena (2014, p.376) review "what we know about companies' choices of how to protect their inventions, which is directly linked with the question of how companies appropriate returns to their innovations." According to these authors, when it comes to intellectual property protection, firms choose between formal mechanisms (patents, trademarks, registered designs, and copyright) and informal mechanisms (secrecy, confidentiality agreements, first mover advantage, or complexity.) They point out that patent protection contributes to knowledge spillovers (via imitation) whereas secrecy "may hinder the circulation of new ideas and therefore slow down knowledge spillovers and economic growth". Additionally, they report that "the available empirical evidence … strongly suggests that only a small fraction of innovative companies relies on patents to protect their inventions" such as biotech firms, while other, such as software companies, do not.

Cooter and Ulen (Chapters 4 and 5), eloquently describe, along with their own, the contributions of Coase (1960), Hobbes (2012) and Calabresi-Melamed (1972) that serve as fundamental guiding principles in a society's continuous effort to improve and establish legal rules that relate to property:

(i) According to *Coase's invariance theorem*, Coase (1960), if property rights are clearly-defined and enforceable and free trades of negative externalities can occur, then private bargaining between property violators and victims will lead to an efficient resolution no matter how property rights are allocated. In other words, when transaction costs (such as search costs, bargaining costs and enforcement costs) are zero, private deals give rise to efficient allocation of resources, irrespective of the legal assignment of property rights.

(ii) Cooter and Ulen offer a corollary of the Coase invariance theorem. According to the *Cooter-Ulen corollary to the Coase theorem*, when transaction costs are high enough to prevent partially or totally effective private dealings, the efficient allocation of recourses will be a function of clearly-defined property rights.

(iii) Calabresi and Melamed have offered two additional corollaries to the Coase invariance theorem regarding compensation and injunction: (a) according to the *first Calabresi-Melamed corollary theorem*, when high transaction costs impede cooperation for the resolution of property disputes, awarding compensatory money damages, through the legal system, would be an efficient remedy; and (b) according to the *second Calabresi-Melamed corollary theorem*, when transaction costs are low, awarding an injunction against a defendant's interference with a plaintiff's property, through the legal system, would be an efficient remedy.

(iv) According to *Coase's normative theorem*, society ought to structure the legal system in such a way so that obstacles to private dealings are minimized or removed, in other words, the law ought to encourage cooperative agreements between property-disputing agents.

(v) Cooter and Ulen point out that Coase's normative theorem stands in contrast to the philosophical believes of Hobbes who doubts that people are capable of rationally dividing a possible cooperative surplus. According to Hobbes, the law ought to avert coercive pressures and eradicate the harmfulness of disagreements. Hence, according to the *normative Hobbes theorem*, the law has to be structured in such a way so that injuries caused by failure in private dealings are minimized. The normative Hobbes theorem implies that the law should assign property claims to the entity that values them the most.

The above theorems center on transaction costs such as search costs, bargaining costs, and enforcement costs. Libecap (2014), addresses transaction costs associated with global environmental externalities; in the author's words (p.428), "in the context of global environmental externality mitigation, four factors raise transactions costs: (1) scientific uncertainty; (2) varying preferences and perceptions; (3) asymmetric information; and (4) lack of compliance and new entry" and stresses that the grater these factors are the less likely it is that there would be agreements on property rights and disputes.

In another seminal contribution Coase (1937) argues that firms exist to minimize transaction costs (to economize on the cost of coordinating economic activity.) Costs of searching markets, inputs, negotiating and signing deals with input suppliers, enforcement of deals, and other such transaction costs give rise to the significance of business firm property boundaries: should the firm own the entire vertical chain associated with the products it produces or just a portion of it? In other words, how many inputs should the firm "make" itself and how many should it "buy" in available markets? How significant are "scale of operations", "input specificity", "frequency of purchase", and "uncertainty"? By and large this contribution of Coase is acknowledged in research that involves the theory of the firm and industrial organization [see Williamson (1985), Kantarelis (2014) and references therein] but, it is ignored by both legal scholars and economists concerned with property issues with the exception of Demsetz (1967) who clearly explains the importance of scale vis-à-vis land ownership settlements and externalities; in his own words:

> *... land was distributed in randomly sized parcels to randomly selected owners. These owners now negotiate among themselves to internalize any remaining externalities. Two market options are open to the negotiators. The first is simply to try to reach a contractual agreement among owners that directly deals with the external effects at issue. The second option is for some owners to buy out others, thus changing the parcel size owned. Which option is selected will depend on which is cheaper. We have here a standard economic problem of optimal scale. If there exist constant returns to scale in the ownership of different sized parcels, it will be largely*

> *a matter of indifference between outright purchase and contractual agreement if only a single, easy-to-police, contractual agreement will internalize the externality. But, if there are several externalities, so that several such contracts will need to be negotiated, or if the contractual agreements should be difficult to police, then outright purchase will be the preferred course of action. The greater the diseconomies of scale to land ownership the more will contractual arrangement be used by the interacting neighbors to settle these differences. Negotiating and policing costs will be compared to costs that depend on the scale of ownership, and parcels of land will tend to be owned in sizes which minimize the sum of these* costs. (*Compare this with the similar rationale given by R. H. Coase to explain the firm in the "The Nature of the Firm", Economics, New Series, 1937, pp. 386-405.)*

Without a doubt, the above theorems as well as Demsetz's analysis, which implies that property rights contribute to more efficient use of resources, serve as fundamental principles in the fields of property law, environmental law, law and economics as well as the business firm and its proprietary domains ranging from physical to intellectual. These authors though do not discuss conditions under which invariance property deals may not materialize due to agents' types (such as strong or weak) and lack of incentive compatibility. For example, in a seller / buyer property deal, both parties may be strong (one asking for a very high market price, the other willing to pay a very low market price) in which case the deal may not be consummated; and if they are both weak, or one weak and the other strong, it is likely that only an incentive-compatible legal ruling (so that the parties do not experience problems associated with asymmetry of information such as adverse selection and moral hazard) can enable the entities to complete the deal. Naturally, the possible types of an agent and the per-type reservation values (threat values) cannot be known with certainty which implies that incentive-compatible legal rulings may contain errors that cause resource misallocation.

My purpose in this chapter is two-fold; firstly, to review the Coasean underpinnings of basic property law and secondly, to propose a broader version of Coase's invariance theorem inclusive of incentive-compatibility. It is my hope that the theorem would be considered more realistic if it is modified to read as follows: when transaction costs (such as search costs, bargaining costs and enforcement costs) are zero, *incentive-compatible deals, mediated by the legal system,* give rise to efficient allocation of resources, irrespective of the legal assignment of property rights. Coase is not concerned about asymmetry of information issues which may give rise to adverse selection and moral hazard. The modification of the theorem, as it will be explained below, amounts to incentive-compatibility subject to knowing the probability distribution of the types of the parties involved (e.g., strong or weak) and to appropriate legal rules that eliminate problems associated with asymmetry of information.

In the following sections of this chapter, I describe the logic of the Coasean invariance theorem and a few possible applications (Section II); I use an example to demonstrate various legal rules subject to Coase, Hobbes and Calabresi-Melamed (Section III); I modify the Coase invariance theorem to include types of agents and incentive compatibility (Section IV); I summarize and conclude in Section V.

II. The Coase invariance theorem

Coase (1960) suggested that a solution to the problem of negative externalities due to environmental pollution is not necessary. Assuming that economic agents are free to negotiate – pollutes (victims) can pay the polluter (violator of property rights) to reduce pollution or the polluter can bribe the pollutees to accept more pollution – Coase showed that the same amount of output and pollution would be produced, regardless of which side owned the rights to clean air or water or, in general, property affected. If the polluter owned the right to clean property, the pollutee would pay until the marginal benefit from emission reduction equaled the marginal cost. If the pollutee owned the right to clean property, the polluter would pay until the marginal cost equaled the marginal benefit of less emission. Hence, with zero or insignificant obstacles to bargaining (zero or insignificant bargaining-related transaction costs), the parties involved would reach the same Pareto optimal levels of output and emission. The only dissimilarity would be an equity issue: who pays whom for the right to make use of the property.

To illustrate Coase's invariance prediction, consider two interdependent economic entities X (the polluter) and Y (the pollutee.) For example, following Cooter and Ulen (p. 94), X may be a coal-based electricity firm and Y a laundry firm in the vicinity. The electricity firm may pay, or get paid by the laundry firm, to install scrubbers; alternatively, the laundry firm may pay, or get paid by the electricity firm, to install air filters.

Following Binger and Hoffman (pp. 565-567), let Π = profit, TR = total revenue, TC = total cost, x= X's output, y = Y's output, L = labor, P = given output price, w = given wage rate, MP = marginal product, and ∂ = symbol for partial derivative.

(a) Suppose first that, by law, Y has the right to be free from pollution and agrees to let X emit pollutants for a per-unit of x fee (k), to be determined by a competitive market.

<u>Firm Y when it is favored by the law</u>

Given P_Y, w and k, Y chooses L_Y and x to maximize profit as follows:

$\Pi_Y = TR_Y - TC_Y$, where

$TR_Y = P_Y y + kx$;

$y = y(L_Y, x)$ or, 'y' is a production function in which y depends positively on L_Y and negatively on x; and

$TC_Y = wL_Y$. Thus,

$$\Pi_Y = P_Y y(L_Y, x) + kx - wL_Y. \qquad (1)$$

The partial derivatives of (1) with respect to L_Y and x are:

$$\frac{\partial \Pi_Y}{\partial L_Y} = P_Y \frac{\partial y}{\partial L_Y} - w = 0$$

$$\frac{\partial \Pi_Y}{\partial x} = P_Y \frac{\partial y}{\partial x} + k = 0$$

From the second partial,

$$k = -P_Y \frac{\partial y}{\partial x}. \qquad (2)$$

<u>Firm X when the law favors Y</u>

Given P_X, w and k, X chooses L_X to maximize profit as follows:

$\Pi_X = TR_X - TC_X$, where

$TR_X = P_X x$;

$x = x(L_X)$ or, 'x' is a production function in which x depends positively on L_X; and

$TC_X = wL_X + k\,x(L_X)$. Thus,

$$\Pi_X = P_X x(L_X) - wL_X - k\,x(L_X). \tag{3}$$

The partial derivative of (3) with respect to L_x is:

$$\frac{\partial \Pi_X}{\partial L_X} = (P_X - k)\frac{\partial x}{\partial L_X} - w = 0,$$

from which,

$$k = P_X - \frac{w}{\dfrac{\partial x}{\partial L_X}}. \tag{4}$$

From (2) and (4),

$$P_X = \frac{w}{\frac{\partial x}{\partial L_X}} - P_Y \frac{\partial y}{\partial x}. \tag{5}$$

(b) Suppose second that, by law, X has the right to pollute and that Y agrees to pay X a per-unit of (x_i - x) bribe (z), to be determined by a competitive market (where x_i = some given, agreed upon, initial output level.)

Firm Y when the law favors X

Given P_Y, w and z, Y chooses L_Y and x to maximize profit as follows:

$\Pi_Y = TR_Y - TC_Y$, where

$TR_Y = P_Y y$;

y = y(L_Y, x) or, as above, 'y' is a production function in which y depends positively on L_Y and negatively on x; and

$TC_Y = wL_Y + z(x_i - x)$. Thus,

$$\Pi_Y = P_Y y(L_Y, x) - wL_Y - z(x_i - x). \tag{6}$$

The partial derivatives of (6) with respect to L_Y and x are:

$$\frac{\partial \Pi_Y}{\partial L_Y} = P_Y \frac{\partial y}{\partial L_Y} - w = 0$$

$$\frac{\partial \Pi_Y}{\partial x} = P_Y \frac{\partial y}{\partial x} + z = 0$$

From the second partial,

$$z = -P_Y \frac{\partial y}{\partial x}. \tag{7}$$

<u>Firm X when it is favored by the law</u>

Given P_x, w and k, X chooses L_x to maximize profit as follows:

$\Pi_X = TR_X - TC_X$, where

$TR_X = P_X x + z[x_i - x(L_X)]$

$x = x(L_X)$ or, as above, 'x' is a production function in which x depends positively on L_X; and

$TC_X = wL_X$. Thus,

$$\Pi_X = P_X x + z[x_i - x(L_X)] - wL_X. \tag{8}$$

The partial derivative of (8) with respect to L_X is:

$$\frac{\partial \Pi_X}{\partial L_X} = (P_X - z)\frac{\partial x}{\partial L_X} - w = 0\,,$$

from which,

$$z = P_X - \frac{w}{\dfrac{\partial x}{\partial L_X}}\,. \tag{9}$$

From (8) and (9),

$$P_X = \frac{w}{\dfrac{\partial x}{\partial L_X}} - P_Y\frac{\partial y}{\partial x}\,. \tag{10}$$

As it may be seen, equation (10) is identical to equation (5), which proves Coase's invariance prediction.

Equation (2) may be viewed as the polutee's marginal damages (MD) set of points, a positively sloped relationship. Similarly, equation (4) may be viewed as the polluter's marginal abatement cost (MAC) set of points, a negatively sloped relationship. Because emission (e) depends on the amount of x produced, the MD, MAC sets may be expressed as functions of "e" and look as those in Figure 1 below. [For more on other possible shapes of the MD/MAC curves as well as more complete analysis see Field (2012)].

Without obstacles to negotiations, X's MAC and Y's MD meet at point B which corresponds to e^*, the overall cost minimizing point. At e^*, total abatement costs for X equal $e_M Be^*$ and total damages for Y equal $e_T Be^*$. Y would prefer e_T, the tolerable level of emissions, and X would prefer e_M, the maximum possible level of emissions, but negotiation would drive them to point e^*. Point e^* may be selected by regulation authorities to serve as a standard (subject to, of course, all possible ailments discussed above.)

The MAC curve may shift to the left due to 'green' technology improvement which, ceteris paribus, will reduce overall emission-related costs for both X and Y. Assuming that regulation authorities desire to enforce e^*, enforcement costs will cause the MAC curve to rotate to the right around point e_M thus contributing to an increase of the overall emission-related costs for both X and Y.

The MD curve may shift to the left (right) due to an increase (decrease) in the population of firms type Y which will contribute to an increase (decrease) of the overall emission-related costs for both X and Y.

Figure 1: Marginal abatement costs and marginal damages

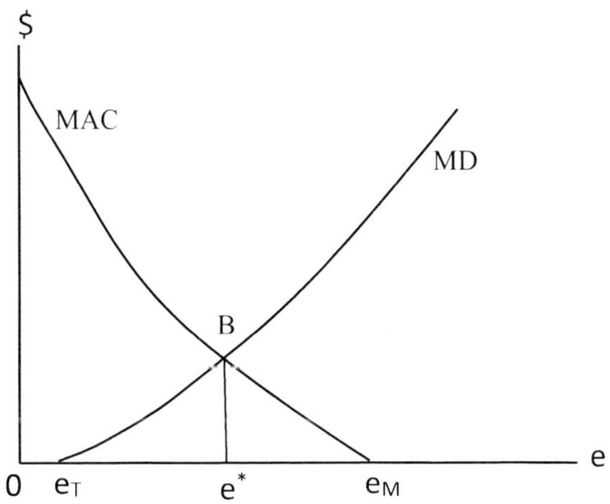

The MAC / MD framework may be utilized to demonstrate the so-called tradable pollution permits. Consider two polluting firms (R and S) whose MAC curves are displayed in Figure 2 and the following two regulation regimes:

(i) Regulation without permits. According to the regulating authority, the two firms should not emit, in total, more than 6 units of the toxic pollutant into the air. Firm R (the firm producing with modern 'green' technology) is currently regulated to emit 4 units of the pollutant while firm S (the firm producing with older 'less green' technology) is currently regulated to emit 2 units of the same pollutant.

Under these regulation requirements, S's total abatement cost is TAC_S = ABC, R's total abatement cost is TAC_R = DFG, and the total abatement cost with no permits (NP) is $TAC_{NP} = TAC_S + TAC_R$.

(ii) Regulation with permits. Alternatively, the regulatory authority may allow firms to negotiate with each other over how much pollutant each is going to emit into the air as long as the total does not exceed the standard of 6 units. Currently, let S emit 2 units and R 4 units; although the total of 6 units satisfies the constraint, under this regulation regime, S and R may agree to the following distribution of emissions: R decreases its emissions from 4 to 3 units and incurs an additional abatement cost of FDLB′; S increases its emission from 2 units to 3 and saves BALB′ in abatement cost. When S and R move to B′, each emits 3 units for a total of 6, which satisfies the standard. Upon comparison of the respective areas in Figure 2, it is obvious that S saves, in absolute value, more than R pays. Hence, S may keep a portion of its savings and with the remaining compensate R so that both end up with more gains while simultaneously satisfy the regulatory constraint. In other words, S purchases a permit from R to emit more for which, of course, R is amply compensated. Hence, regulation with permits enables both firms to earn more - and society to improve - while, concurrently, firms satisfy the regulatory emission standard. Comparing the outcomes of schemes (i) and (ii), in conjunction with Figure 2, regulation with permits (WP) reduces total abatement costs more than no permit regulation (NP): $TAC_{WP} < TAC_{NP}$.

Figure 2: The importance of pollution permits

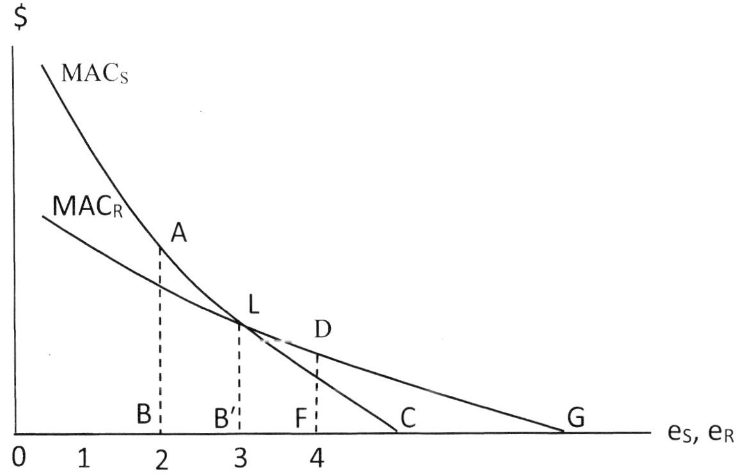

III. Alternative legal rules and their impact

The Coase, Hobbes and Calabresi-Melamed theorems may be used in conjunction with a hypothetical numerical example (similar to an example that appears in Cooter and Ulen) to demonstrate the impact of alternative legal rules.

Let there be two agents, a polluter (E) and a pollutee (L); E emits a pollutant which negatively affects L's payoffs. E has available two strategies: abate effluence (A), do not abate effluence (NA); similarly, L has available two strategies: pay E not to pollute or protect against E's effluence (P), do not pay E or do not protect against E's effluence (NP). The matrix below displays the payoffs of the two agents (E plays left, L plays right). Would it be optimal to structure the law so that we achieve the maximum possible for society, in this case, the total payoffs (3150) that correspond to the Nash equilibrium of (NA, P)?

L

E

	NP	P
NA	2500, 550	2500, 650
A	980, 880	980, 650

Let us know consider the implications of the following three rules of law and the table below:

Rules of law:

- Rule I: E is free to pollute.
- Rule II: L is entitled to compensatory damages from E.
- Rule III: L is entitled to an injunction forbidding E to pollute.

According to Rule I, it would be optimal for E to adopt strategy NA and make 2500 while it would optimal for L to adopt strategy P and make 650 for a society total of 3150. Hence, society would be indifferent between non-cooperation (Hobbes) or cooperation (Coase).

According to Rule II, L would adopt NP to make 880, the highest possible in that column. E has two choices A or NA. If E chooses A it would make 980; if it chooses NA it will make 2500 and L will make 550. Since L is entitled to compensatory damages from E, E would have the incentive to choose NA and then compensate L for the difference between (880-550) so that it ends up with 2170 and L with 880. Hence, if cooperation is not possible, society would realize a total of 3050 with a leftover of 100. But, if Coasean cooperation is possible, E and L may negotiate to split (evenly or unevenly) the leftover for a total of 3150, the maximum possible that society may realize. (In the table below the left over is evenly split.)

According to Rule III, E cannot pollute. Therefore, E would realize 980 while L will realize 880 for a non-cooperative total of 1860 and a leftover of 1290. But, if Coasean cooperation is possible, E and L may negotiate to split (evenly or unevenly) the leftover for a total of 3150, the maximum possible that society may realize. (In the table below the left over is evenly split.)

	Cooperation not possible (Hobbes)		Leftover	Cooperation possible (Coase)		Total à la Coase
	E	L		E	L	E + L
Rule I	2500	650	0	2500	650	3150
Rule II	2170	880	100	2220	930	3150
Rule III	980	880	1290	1625	1525	3150

The numerical example demonstrates the power of the Coase invariance theorem when the parties involved do not experience any obstacles to cooperation: in the face of well-defined property rights, no matter how the law is structured, society ends up with the maximum possible which also corresponds to the Nash equilibrium in this case. The example also demonstrates the power of the Hobbes theorem when obstacles to cooperation exist as well as the value of the Calabresi-Melamed compensatory and injunction rules as applied to property rights violations.

IV. Information asymmetry

As the above examples demonstrate, the Coase theorem does not take into consideration the possibility of information asymmetry when parties, in the absence of transaction costs, bargain for prices or compensation. According to the theorem the price or compensation agreed upon by the parties is fair; hence, conveniently, there is no need to address the possibility of information asymmetry.

However, with zero transaction costs and information asymmetry, depending on the type of each negotiating party (strong or weak), (a) a property dispute may not be consummated and (b) a negotiator in a bilateral property dispute, void of incentive-compatibility, may lie and thus receive an exploitative price which, afterwards, may cause costly litigation for all involved. For example, in a bilateral property dispute, one party may be strong and ask for an extremely high price and the other party may be equally strong and offer to pay an extremely low price; in such a case, the parties may not come to an agreement despite zero transaction costs and, since the types of the disputing parties are fixed - not merely obstacles that may be removed or minimized - the normative Coase theorem does not apply either. But even if one party is strong and the other weak, only an incentive-compatible agreement may contribute to the validity of a deal by totally eliminating adverse selection and moral hazard. [2]

According to Myerson (2008, p. 587), in economic life we ought to constantly search for ways to improve the pool of resources and for incentive mechanisms. Hayek (1945) recommended that a social institution (such as the market system) should be viewed as a mechanism for communicating people's information and coordinating people's actions. In a market system, the actions of a market participant depend on *information* provided by other participants and on the ability of the system to coordinate the participants towards an economic outcome (preferably Pareto optimum). Is *information* truthful? Do participants have the incentive to lie and / or disobey? If they do, how can we make them tell the truth and obey? Following Myerson, consider the following example: suppose a buyer and a seller (both risk-neutral, and expected profit maximizes) are willing to trade property; their types (known only to them) are "strong" and "weak" each with a probability of 0.5. Obviously, if both the buyer and the seller are strong, trade between the two would not take place. Table 1 below reports threat values, or reservations prices, according to types (buyer: \$20, \$120; seller: \$80, \$10). In the cells, numbers to the left of the comma (denoted by p_A, p_B, p_C, p_D) correspond to the probabilities that trade will take place in those cells; numbers to the right of the comma (denoted by $A, $B, $C, $D) correspond to dollar figures based on different types.

Table 1: Bilateral Setting

			Buyer's type and threat value	
			Strong (0.5)	Weak (0.5)
			$20	$120
Seller's type and threat value	Strong (0.5)	$80	p_A, \$A	p_B, \$B
	Weak (0.5)	$10	p_C, \$C	p_D, \$D

Consider now a Fifty / Fifty Split bilateral agreement in Table 2 according to which the price agreed upon is half the sum of the corresponding threat values.

Table 2: Fifty / Fifty Split Agreement

			Buyer's type and threat value	
			Strong (0.5)	Weak (0.5)
			$20	$120
Seller's type and threat value	Strong (0.5)	$80	0, No Trade	1, $100
	Weak (0.5)	$10	1, $15	1, $65

Let w = weak seller, s = strong seller, and ws = weak seller who pretends to be strong.

If the seller is weak, her expected profit would be:

$E(\Pi)w = (15 - 10)(1)(0.5) + (65 - 10)(1)(0.5) = 30.$

If the seller is weak but pretends to be strong, her expected profit would be:

$E(\Pi)ws = (100 - 10)(1)(0.5) = 45.$

Thus, because $E(\Pi)ws > E(\Pi)w$, the seller has the incentive to lie. Similarly, the buyer has the incentive to lie since her $E(\Pi)w = 37.5 < E(\Pi)ws = 52.5$.

Therefore, given the above setting, the Fifty / Fifty Split bilateral agreement is not incentive compatible which implies that deal cannot be consummated.

Consider now a possible Incentive-Compatible bilateral agreement in conjunction with Table 3. The cells, as above, contain probabilities and prices, where q is a conditional probability of trade applied to the respective cells; the conditional probability for (weak, weak) remains 1. According to Myerson (p. 591), "the probability of trade could also be interpreted as the conditional expected number of objects that the buyer would get in this case, and so $q \leq 1$ here can also be interpreted as a *resource constraint*, expressing the fact that there is only one object that they can trade; … for a strong trader to participate in this plan, y must satisfy the *participation constraint*", in this case $y \leq 10$. Thus, appropriate values of "q" and "y" will generate incentive compatibility.

Table 3: Incentive-Compatible Split Agreement

			Buyer's type and threat value	
			Strong (0.5)	Weak (0.5)
			$20	$120
Seller's type and threat value	Strong (0.5)	$80	0, No Deal	q, $120-y
	Weak (0.5)	$10	q, $10+y	1, $65

Proceeding as above, if the seller is weak, her expected profit would be:

$$E(\Pi)w = (10 + y - 10)(q)(0.5) + (65 - 10)(1)(0.5) = 0.5qy + 27.5.$$

If the seller is weak but pretends to be strong, her expected profit would be:

$$E(\Pi)ws = (120 - y - 10)(q)(0.5) = 55q - 0.5qy.$$

Thus, to make honesty an equilibrium, q and y must satisfy the informational constraint

$$0.5qy + 27.5 \geq 55q - 0.5qy.$$

Solving for q,

$q \leq 27.5/(55 - y)$.

Therefore, the incentive constraints $\mathbf{q \leq 27.5/(55 - y)}$ and $\mathbf{y \leq 10}$ can generate an infinite number of possible incentive-compatible agreements. Similarly, for the buyer.

These agreements, of course, need a legal environment within which they may be arbitrated and if needed litigated and enforced. Hence, if informational asymmetry is prevalent, even with zero transaction costs, Coase's invariance prediction may hold only if the property-disputing parties (a) are aware of the role that their uncertain "types" may play (which may cause a deal not to be consummated) and (b) are capable of drafting adverse selection free and moral hazard free incentive-compatible and legally enforceable rules (not an easy task.) Hence, given the theoretical exploration endeavored in this section, Coase's invariance theorem may be stated, more broadly, as follows: *when transaction costs (such as search costs, bargaining costs and enforcement costs) are zero, incentive-compatible deals, mediated by the legal system, give rise to efficient allocation of resources, irrespective of the legal assignment of property rights.*

V. Summary & Conclusion

I made an attempt above to modify the Coase theorem as applied to property law by bringing into the argument asymmetry of information (ignored by Coase) and point out that, even without transaction costs, uncertainty over the types of property-disputing parties and the difficulty in drafting efficient deals may cause adverse selection and moral hazard or unstable resolutions due to incentive incompatibility. My argument does not reject the theorem; it serves as a complement by adding the importance of (a) "types" of negotiators and (b) incentive-compatibility in environments characterized by asymmetry in information. Thus, for the theorem's invariance prediction to hold we have to assume zero transaction costs, knowledge of the probability distribution of agents' types, and capability in drafting incentive-compatible agreements.

I would like to conclude by raising some questions for possible future research:

(1) High property taxes in a certain town (primarily to support high quality public education) may cause emigration of low income people to other towns with lower property taxes where high population density may negatively affect the quality of public services (such as public education and sanitation) and contribute to the deterioration of housing as well as to the emergence of gang activity and lawlessness. In this case, could the receiving town, where the underprivileged move, become a *tragedy of the commons*

region due to property rights misallocation which satisfies the utilitarian objectives of some at the expense of everyone else? Could incentive-compatible agreements between privilege and underprivileged members enable society to eradicate such tragedy of the commons and, as Singer (2000, p.25) points out, build a "bridge between the haves and the have-nots"? In my judgment, Singer (p.36), thoughtfully guides us on how to select criteria for the effective engineering of incentive-compatible rulings; in his words, "it is the job of the law to manage tensions between competing interests in access and exclusion, change and stability, wealth and equality, liberty and security. The question for us all is: what values should inform us as we choose property rules and institutions? How should the law shape economic and social life?"

(2) Lack of property rights in developing nations, caused by past historic property misallocations owing to asymmetry in information and the resultant deception and exploitation of local populations, have given rise to informal firms which hinder economic development and growth. According to the United Nations (2008, p.1) "four billion people around the world are robbed of the chance to better their lives and climb out of poverty, because they are excluded from the rule of law due to business informality." Obviously citizens in these countries need property rights or titles. Referencing De Soto (2000), Kantarelis (p.10) states that "informal business firms account for up to about half of economic activity in developing nations ... and are held back by barriers to official recognition: lack of secure property titles, deeds, securities and

contracts that describe the economically significant aspects of assets. The lowering of such barriers would improve the ability of firms to borrow against registered and secured property-based collateral; additionally, it would enable them to more easily acquire, and / or merge with, other firms." Unfortunately, the informality problem persists despite the various efforts being made, which indicates how difficult it is to engineer incentive-compatible agreements in order to remove barriers to property ownership. As Singer (p. 91) emphasizes, "[p]roperty is not just about self-interest. It is about creating the ground rules for fair social relationships."

Endnotes

1. Sen (p.12) tells the charming story of three children, Anne, Bob, and Carla, who are arguing over the property rights to a flute. Anne claims ownership of the flute on the basis that she is the only one able to play it; Bob claims it because he, unlike the other children, has no other toys to play with; Carla claims the flute since it was stolen from her after she made it with her own hands. Based on different philosophical beliefs, all three property claims can be taken to be reasonable. Sen's point is that one can produce intuitively believable reasons for assigning property of the flute to any one of the children. Hence, utilitarians - and "for more worthy ends" Aristotelians - would favor Anne, egalitarians Bob, and libertarians Carla. The point here is that there is no reason to assume, as Rawls and most of his followers do, that we have to decide which one of these claims is fairest or most just (Rawls, 1985). Of course, one may wonder: what if the 'flute' were a 'Stradivarius violin'?

2. The problem of getting to share information honestly is called adverse selection. The problem of getting people to act obediently to a plan is called moral hazard.

References

Binger, B.R. and Hoffman, E. (1988), *Microeconomics with Calculus*, Scott Foresman.

Calabresi, G. and Melamed, A. D. (1972), "Property Rules, Liability Rules, and Inalienability: One View of the Cathedral," *Harvard Law Review*, Vol. 85, pp: 1089-1128.

Coase, R. (1937), "The Nature of the Firm", *Economica*, Vol.4, pp: 386-405.

Coase, R. (1960), "The Problem of Social Cost", *Journal of Law and Economics*, Vol.3, pp: 1-44.

Cooter, R. & Ulen, T. (1996), *Law and Economics, 2nd ed.*, Addison-Wesley.

Demsetz, H. (1967), "Toward a Theory of Property Rights," *American Economic Review Papers & Proceedings*, Vol.57, pp: 347-359.

De Soto, H. (2000), *The Mystery of Capital: Why Capitalism Triumphs in the West and Fails Everywhere Else*, Basic Books.

Eswaran, M. & H. M. Neary (2014), "An Economic Theory of the Evolutionary Emergence of Property Rights", *American Economic Journal: Microeconomics*, Vol. 6, #3, pp: 203-226.

Field, B. C. & M. K. Field (2012), *Environmental Economics: An Introduction, 6th ed.*, McGraw-Hill

Hall, B., Helmers, C., Rogers, M., & V. Sena, "The Choice between Formal and Informal Intellectual Property: A Review:, *Journal of Economic Literature*, Vol LII, #2, pp: 375-423.

Hayek, Friedrich A. (1945), "The Use of Knowledge in Society", *American Economic Review*, Vol XXXV, #4, pp: 519-30.

Hobbes, T. (2012), *Leviathan,* edited by Noel Malcolm, Oxford University Press.

Kantarelis, D. (2014), *Theories of the Firm, 4th ed.*, Inderscience.

Libecap, G. D. (2014), "Addressing Global Environmental Externalities: Transaction Costs Considerations", *Journal of Economic Literature*, Vol LII, #2, pp: 424-479.

Myerson, Roger B. (2008), "Perspectives on Mechanism Design in Economic Theory", *American Economic Review*, Vol 98, #3, pp: 586-603.

Rawls, J. (1985), "Justice as Fairness: Political not Metaphysical", *Philosophy and Public Affairs*, Vol. 14, pp: 223-251.

Sen, Amartya (2009), *The Idea of Justice*, Harvard University Press.

Singer, Joseph W. (2000), *The Edges of the Field*, Beacon Press, Boston.

United Nations, (2008), "Making the Law Work for Everyone", *Report of the Commission on Legal Empowerment of the Poor, United Nations*, Vol. 1, 2008.

Williamson, O. (1985), *The Economic Institutions of Capitalism*, Free Press.

Chapter 2:

Contracts

I. Introduction and literature review

Incomplete information, global markets, reputation and even behavioral issues complicate contract writing to say the least, making management of deals a business function of paramount importance. In addition to the constant quest for competitive advantage, how does the firm manage risk associated with promisor-type and promisee-type deals with various internal and external agents? Although, this risk may be minimized through portfolio of deals diversification, such a possibility has been overlooked by scholars in law, business, and economics despite the many between the lines hints offered in the literature.

Transaction cost theories of the firm [Coase (1937), Williamson (1985)] and other theories described by Kantarelis (2010)] center around the extreme choices of markets and hierarchies for organizing economic activity. However,

Table 1: Dimensions of transactions and governance structures [*]

CRITICAL DIMENSIONS OF TRANSACTIONS		VERTICAL INTEGRATION	ALLIANCES & JOINT VENTURES	MARKET USE
Input Specificity	High	√		
	Low	√ If low cost allies or suppliers do not exist [**]	√ If low cost allies may be found [**]	√ If low cost suppliers exist [**]
Frequency of Transactions	High			√
	Low	√	√ If trustworthy allies may be found	
Uncertainty about values of resources over time	High	√ If concern is not shared	√ If concern is shared	
	Low			√

[*] "√" indicates choice.

[**] These are allies or suppliers that experience economies of scale.

intermediate forms of governance exist, called hybrids, which according to Masten (1996, p.12) "combine contracting and vertical integration or lie somewhere between markets and hierarchy in terms of incentive intensity, adaptability and bureaucratic costs." Hybrids are the result of, among other, mergers, strategic alliances as well as joint ventures and they are affected by various contracts and deals, legal systems, governmental regulations and even cultures. In a self-explanatory fashion, Table 1 displays the three dimensions of transactions discussed by Williamson (1985) in conjunction with choices associated with three possible governance structures: vertical integration, some hybrids (alliances and joint ventures) and market use.

Although a contract is a very effective instrument that a firm may use to maintain and enhance its profit-making ability, the picture sketched in Table 1 and popular theories of the firm [Neoclassical, Transaction Cost, Principal-Agent, Evolutionary – see Kantarelis (2010)] neglect to explicitly inform us about the importance of contracts. As many authors have pointed out, incomplete contracts management, contracting party's reputation, irrationality and even psychology may all assist in the pursuit of profit.

According to Rendon (2006, abstract),

> *The contract management process is growing in importance as outsourcing continues to increase and suppliers become virtual extensions of our organization's*

competence and capability. Yet, recent studies indicate that organizations are not managing the contracting process as the core competency that it is, nor are they achieving the strategic competitive advantage resulting from a mature contracting process.

Kim and Mahoney (2010, p. 806) define the firm as a nexus of incomplete contracts "which allows for entrepreneurial alertness, creativity, and judgment under uncertainty" and they emphasize that "the contracting process is a discovery process and entrepreneurial in nature, allowing firms to sense and seize new economic opportunities."

Beuve and Saussier (2012, p. 811), analyzed 3700 inter-firm contractual relationships, based on a sample of French firms, to conclude that "cooperation is enhanced by a partner's reputation".

Sgourev and Zuckerman (2011, p. 3) convincingly argue that although rationality calls sometimes for breach of contract, "short-term emotions [may] overwhelm rational calculation [and that often] a sense of loyalty … leads one to [irrationally] incorporate others' interests into one's own".

O'Reilly III and Main (2010, p. 675) bring into the picture the importance of psychology in relation to CEO compensation as an important factor missing from principal-agent models. As they conclude, based on empirical outcomes,

> *there are strong interaction effects among social influence variables and the social setting of boardroom activity. Generous pay awards, bearing only a weak connection to corporate performance, are explained in the context of the social psychology of the boardroom. These results .... suggest the need for a more comprehensive model of executive compensation that incorporates both economic and psychological determinants*

As stressed by the above authors, incomplete information, global markets, reputation and even behavioral issues complicate contract writing to say the least, making management of contracts a business function of paramount importance; perhaps time has arrived for a theory of the firm that centers on contracts.

Contracts, of course, can be formal, informal, relational, written, verbal, or other, and they must be designed in such a way so that they contribute to the well-being of the contracting parties and, if possible, to other stakeholders. Firms may rely on real world incomplete contracts, which offer both benefits (e.g., protection against opportunism) and costs (e.g., costs associated with transactions, drafting, litigation and misfitism.) If incomplete contracts carry with them more costs than benefits, the parties, instead, may decide to rely on deals.

I would like to define *deal* as a reciprocal duty subject to incentives, reputation, ethics, cultural norms, circumstances, and essential legal elements such as (among many more): offer-acceptance-consideration, capacity of parties, free consent, lawful object, certainty, possibility of performance, not expressly declared void, writing and registration.

Deals may be more effective than ordinary contracts in today's global environment characterized by, traditional firms, service firms, knowledge firms, escalating complexity and rising international competition. Because of the variety and complexity of hybrid forms the firm may be viewed as a function of deals instead of contracts. Deals encompass a wider range of contingencies and as such they may evolve more efficiently, effectively and flexibly.

Deals, like traditional contracts, are about intra- and inter-group, more or less specific relationships that aim to contribute to a firm more than the firm could gain on its own. Deals differ from traditional contracts in that they are more adaptation-intensive, less change resisting; they establish a framework (written or unwritten) within which firms may move more freely in their quest for information to lessen uncertainty and asymmetry and to more successfully cope with change and competition (e.g., breaching under a deal may be less costly than under a traditional contract). As the business / economics environment optimizes and as it naturally selects business blueprints suitable to the environment that firms operate in, it simultaneously selects the deals that govern relationships between firms. Deals that are naturally selected are fit for survival, they need less policing, are less prone to opportunism and are subject to lower costs.

Microfinancing, started by Muhammad Yunus (Peace Nobel Laureate 2006) and his Grameen Bank in Bangladesh to help desperately poor people, might serve as an example of a 'deal'. The bank is built on principles that run counter to the conventional wisdom of western banking (i.e., adaptation to the local social environment.) It seeks out the poorest borrowers, and it requires no collateral for small loans (unheard of in developed nations.) The bank rests on the strength of its borrowers who are primarily women; women are less likely to "flee" or deviate from the deal; unlike men, women are less mobile in Bangladesh and more emotionally attached to their own children, extended families and localities. They are required to join the bank in small self-formed groups. The group members provide one another with peer discipline and support in the form of mutual assistance and advice. By and large, the conditions for a loan are as follows:

- lend small amounts of money to independent investors in small groups (of 4 to 6), without collateral, subject to:
  M = Success Fee or Interest Rate (borrower pays if project succeeds), and
  F = Joint-Liability Fee (borrower pays if a group mate fails);
- choose M and F appropriately to attract safe investors (avoidance of adverse selection); and

- make F sufficiently high so that group mates have the incentive to monitor each other (avoidance of moral hazard).

At the end, without the need for a traditional signed contract, the policing (enforcing) of such a contract or significant administration costs, the deal does more for each than each could do on her own while simultaneously it contributes to the economic development of the region and the nation.

In whatever follows in this chapter I would like to propose that a firm may be viewed as a function of deals (section II) and point out (in section III) that deals may be managed as a portfolio of investments. In section IV, I discuss some factors that govern the effectiveness and efficiency of deals, namely: mediation; credibility; multi-period deals; optimal commitments; efficient default terms; repair malfunctions by regulating the conditions of deals; offer, acceptance, consideration and meeting of minds. In section V, I summarize and conclude.

II. The firm as a function of deals

Reve (1990) views the firm as a nexus of contracts but he does not distinguish between "contracts" and "deals". Following Reve's logic, but viewing the firm as a function of deals, the following set of functions may be justified:

$$\textbf{Firm} = \gamma(\textbf{Deals}) \qquad (1)$$

where

$$\text{Deals} = \delta(\text{Expertise, Inducements}).$$

Expertise and inducements may be found inside the firm as well as outside. Therefore, equation (1) may be expressed as follows:

$$\textbf{Firm} = \varepsilon(\textbf{Internal Deals, External Deals}) \qquad (2)$$

where

$$\text{Internal Deals} = \zeta(\text{Nucleus Expertise, Organizational Inducements}) = \zeta(\text{Strategic Nucleus})$$

and

$$\text{External Deals} = \eta(\text{Matching Expertise, Interorganizational Inducements}) = \eta(\text{Strategic Federation})$$

where, 'Federation' stands for mergers (vertical, horizontal, conglomerate), alliances and joint ventures.

Hence, equation (2), finally, may be expressed as follows:

Firm = λ(Strategic Nucleus, Strategic Federation). (3)

The nucleus expertise of the firm is the firm's formula for competitive advantage or, in the words of Reve (p. 141), it "is the raison d'etre of the firm". This formula is subject to (a) protection, (b) constant efforts for improvement to better adapt to business environments and (c) evolution for creative destruction (Kantarelis, 2003). According to Reve (p. 140), the nucleus expertise is due to asset specificity of four types: location specificity (resource immobility), physical asset specificity (technical and scientific advantages), human asset specificity (knowledge or know-how advantages) and committed assets (specialized investments.)

A federation competes in the 'horizontal' front (against potential entrants with substitute products and services) in the 'vertical' front (for upstream and downstream entities) and in the 'conglomerate' front (for more diversification and access to new arenas.)

Consider Figure 1. A firm consists of three layers: the inner most layer of strategic nucleus, the middle layer due to mergers, and the outer most layer due to alliances and joint ventures. These three layers are connected to various other firms in other industries through conglomerate-type agreements. The 'glue' that keeps this federation together is *deals*, which spread the firm vertically (solid arrow, north to south), horizontally (broken arrow, west to east) and conglomerately (dotted arrow).

Figure 1: Federation

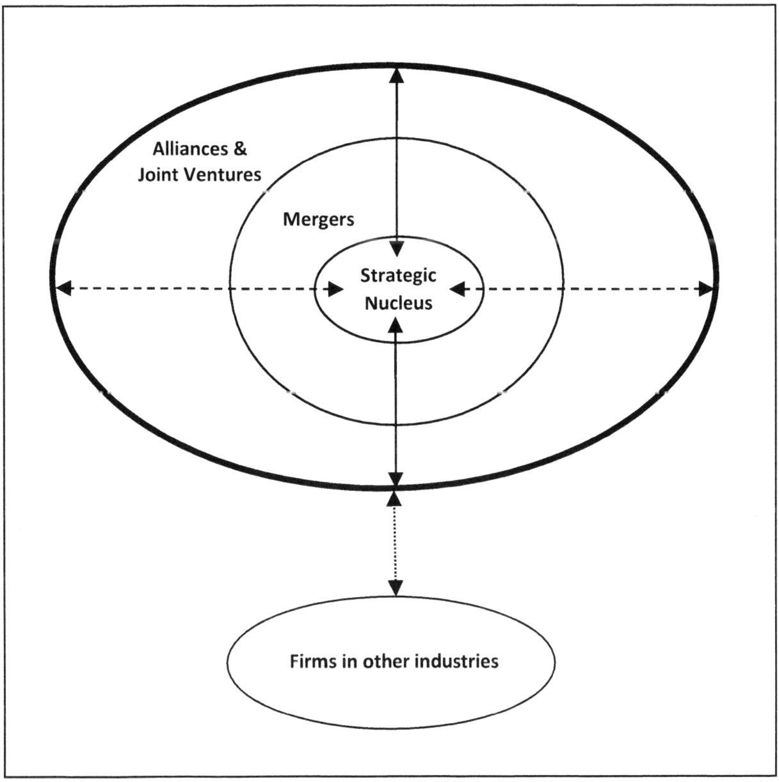

III. Portfolio of deals

Profit-making firms make promisor-type and promisee-type deals. As promisor the firm makes promises and commits resources to performance in an effort to fulfill such promises; as a promisee it relies on promises offered by other firms (e.g., input providers) and commits resources in anticipation of the promised services / goods.

To illustrate, consider a deal for renovation between X (a building construction company) and Y (the owner of a hospital building in need of renovation and extension).[1] To fulfill the promise, X may have to invest, in advance, in specific construction equipment offered by Z, which it does not currently possess. In anticipation of the final project, Y may invest, in advance as well, in additional inputs to offer contracted medical services to constituency W. Obviously, X and Y would be fully interdependent upon each other and the possibility of breaching would motivate them to consider possible compensation remedies with different incentive implications for investments in performance and reliance. At the end, in the deal, the promisor and the promisee should include optimal commitments to performance and reliance. Optimality, of course, requires accurate estimation of damages and it may involve third parties such as private arbitrators, courts or even government representatives.

The firm here is viewed as an entity that makes both types of deals which are assumed to be evolving; in the above illustration, X invests in both performance (to fulfill the contract with Y) and reliance (in anticipation of performance by Z). Similarly, Y invests in performance (to fulfill the contract with W) and reliance (in anticipation of performance by X). The firm's cost may be viewed as the sum of performance cost and reliance cost which may be neutralized due to possible remuneration for damages.

Each deal contributes to profit and contract profit shares are assumed known to the firm. To run its operations, assume for simplicity and without loss of generality, that the firm relies on only two contracts (i and j) and that the respective profit shares are $(\pi_i \mid \pi)$ and $(\pi_j \mid \pi)$ where π = profit; obviously,

$$\left(\frac{\pi_i}{\pi}\right)+\left(\frac{\pi_j}{\pi}\right)=1 \qquad (4)$$

As a further assumption, the firm should consider each contracting partner's reliability (R) where R is a random variable. For simplicity, let R vary as follows: $0 \leq R \leq 1$, where R=0 implies unreliable contracting entity and R = 1 implies perfectly reliable contracting entity. R depends on available first-hand experience, history and reputation information of clients (for promisor-type deals) and input providers (for promisee-type deals). Naturally, R is subject to asymmetry of information and it may be estimated based on first-hand experience, history, reputation, intelligence gathering and / or other. Additionally, a firm's performance as a promisor, and its reliance as a promisee, may be affected by outside factors such unexpected natural phenomena, political risk, war and so on. Hence, for a firm with two contracts, where E(R) = expected reliability and σ^2 = variance,

$$0 \leq R_i \leq 1,\ E(R_i),\ \sigma_i^2 \quad \text{and} \quad 0 \leq R_j \leq 1,\ E(R_j),\ \sigma_j^2 \qquad (5)$$

Given (4) and (5), the firm may attempt to maximize total expected profit, E(π), and minimize contract risk expressed as variance, σ_C^2, where ρ_{ij} =correlation:

$$E(\pi) = \left(\frac{\pi_i}{\pi}\right)E(R_i) + \left(\frac{\pi_j}{\pi}\right)E(R_j) \tag{6}$$

and

$$\sigma_C^2 = \left(\frac{\pi_i}{\pi}\right)^2 \sigma_i^2 + \left(\frac{\pi_j}{\pi}\right)^2 \sigma_j^2 + 2\left(\frac{\pi_i}{\pi}\right)\left(\frac{\pi_j}{\pi}\right)\sigma_i \sigma_j \rho_{ij} \tag{7}$$

Graphing (6) and (7), with (6) on the vertical axis, and various correlation coefficients we may derive deal efficient frontiers (DEF) such as those in Figure 2.

The firm may manage (diversify) its portfolio of deals like an investing firm manages its portfolio of risky assets, as modeled by Markowitz (1959), Treynor (1962) and Lintner (1965). Obviously, moving in the direction of the arrows is always preferred; the lower the correlation the further to the left the DEF moves offering the possibility of higher expected profit at lower risk.

"0" correlation: the firm minimizes risk at K and improve expected profit by moving to the right of K assuming it can afford more risk (similarly with "+1" correlation.) But, if it is located to the left of K on the same "0" correlation frontier, it may move towards K, improve expected profit and lower risk.

Figure 2: Deal Efficient Frontiers

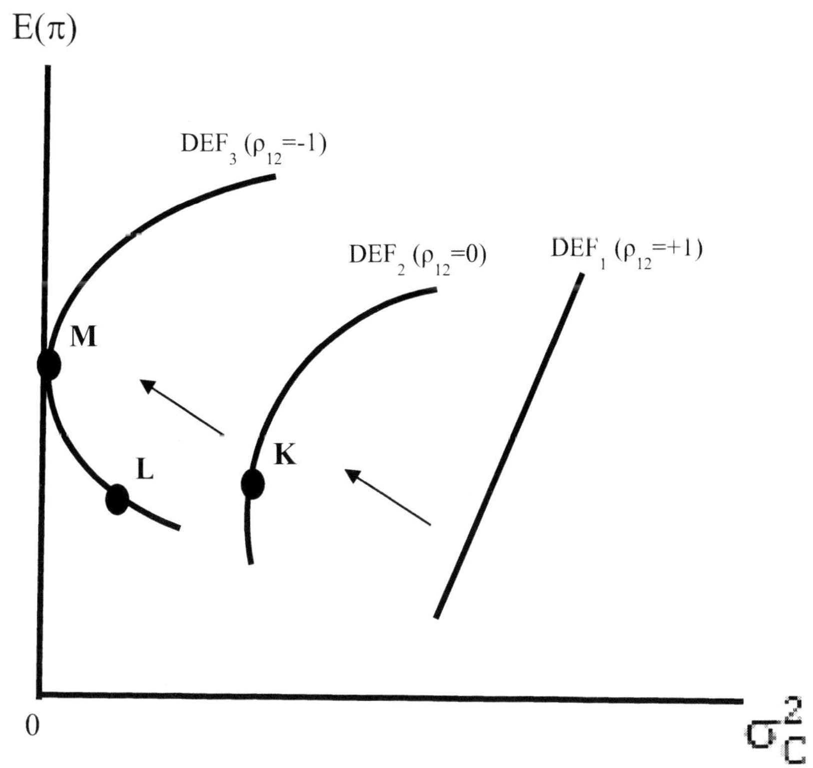

"-1" correlation: if the firm is initially at L it can move to M and improve profit and totally eliminate risk; as above, it can improve profit by moving to the right of M at higher risk.

A move from to L to M may be accomplished via adjustment of profit shares by the firm: for example, suppose at L, i's profit share is 60% and j's profit share is 40%; at M, suppose i's profit share is 70% and j's profit share is 30%; to move from L to M, the firm may devote more energy into the contractual relationship with i (e.g., new terms and negotiations) to bring about a rise in profit share and less energy into the contractual relationship with j for lower profit share.[2]

As alluded above, deals (by being more adaptable and less restrictive with respect to breach and modification) would be easier to manage for the purpose of risk reduction through diversification than rigidly structured traditional contracts. Let me also reiterate, as equation (3) above clearly points out, that the firm may not only rely on deals (internal or external) for more profit but also, and more importantly, on its competitive advantage, its unique nucleus expertise without which it would luck identification, a sense of purpose or vision. Deals must not compromise the firm's nucleus expertise; instead, deals ought to serve as complements to profit-seeking.

IV. Factors that govern the effectiveness and efficiency of deals

In some market exchanges, especially those that involve spot markets, have less need for formal or informal deals. In other markets though, as explained by Cooter and Ulen (1996, pp.168–202), exchanges may involve *payment today for service later*, or *service today for payment later* or *service later for payment later*. Naturally, exchanges that require deferment of service or payment, would need more drafted (internally or externally, more or less formal) deals with the potential to enhance effectiveness of delivery and efficiency of service. Consider below seven (out of many) factors that may govern deals (not necessarily in the order described below or summarized in Flow Chart 1.)

Flow Chart 1: Factors that govern deals

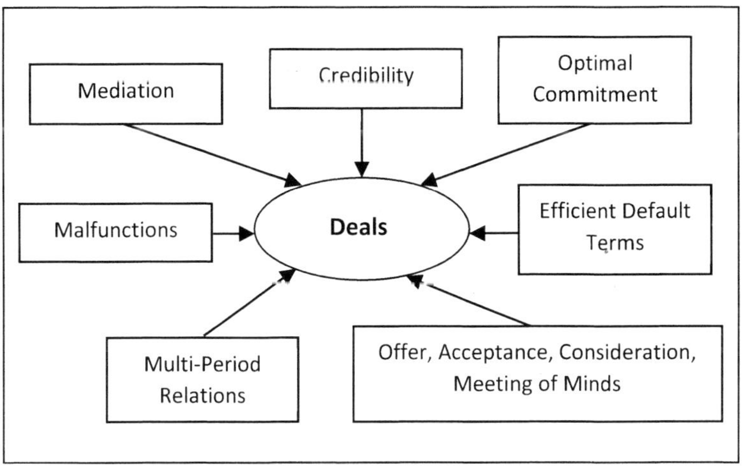

Factor 1 – Mediation

According to Myerson (2008, p. 587), mechanism design can expand "our general view of the economic problem to include incentive constraints as well as resource constraints". Hayek (1945) recommended that a social institution (such as the market system) should be viewed as a mechanism for communicating people's information and coordinating people's actions. In a market system, the actions of a market participant depend on *information* provided by other participants and on the ability of the system to coordinate the participants towards an economic outcome (preferably Pareto optimum).

Is *information* truthful? Would participants share information honestly so that they do not experience adverse selection prior to a deal? And, would they act obediently to a deal so that they do not experience moral hazard after a deal is made? (Figure 3 summarizes definitions and sketches the importance of these questions in relation to time). What may be a feasible and desirable deal and how can we make the contracting parties implement it?

Figure 3: Information asymmetry (t=time)

- **Adverse Selection**:
  the problem of getting to share information honestly prior to a deal
- **Moral Hazard**:
  the problem of getting people to act obediently to a deal

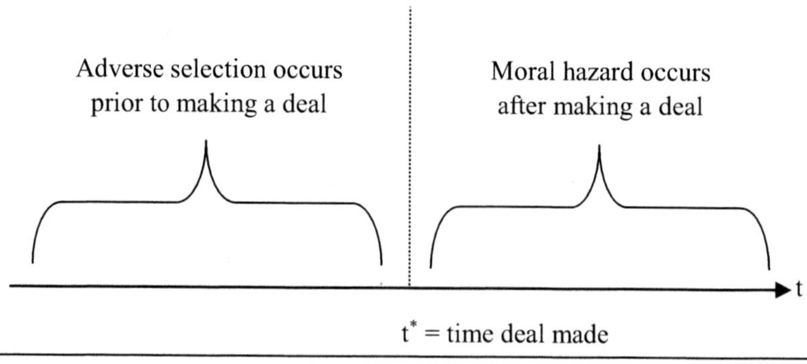

Consider the following example, similar to the one in chapter 1 and to Myerson's (2008): suppose a buyer and a seller (both risk-neutral, and expected profit maximizes) are willing to trade for an input so that nobody becomes worse off; their types (known only to them) are "Strong" and "Weak" each with a probability of 0.5. Obviously if both the buyer and the seller are strong, trade between the two would not take place. Table 2 displays values (private valuations or reservation prices) prior to a deal or before trade.

Table 2: Before trade

			Buyer's type & value	
			Strong (0.5)	Weak (0.5)
			$40	$120
Seller's type & value	Strong (0.5)	$100		
	Weak (0.5)	$10		

Obviously, no trade can take place when the traders are both strong; but, if they are not, they can trade subject to a "split the difference" mediation[3] deal or as indicated in the matrix below (where, in each cell, the number on the left is the probability of trade taking placc and thc numbcr on thc right is thc avcragc of thc reservation prices that correspond to the cell).

(1) Would this mediation deal work?

(2) If not, what mediation constraints may be introduced to make the traders honestly trade with each other?

Coordination Mechanism One: Split-the-Difference deal

Trade whenever the buyer's value is more than the seller's value, and the recommended price is always halfway between their two values.

Table 3 displays the implied results of this split-the-difference deal. In each cell, the number on the right is the price to trade at; the number on the left is the conditional probability that the trade in that cell will take place.

Table 3: Split-the Difference Mediation Deal

			Buyer's type & value	
			Strong (0.5)	Weak (0.5)
			$40	$120
Seller's type & value	Strong (0.5)	$100	0, No trade	1, $110
	Weak (0.5)	$10	1, $25	1, $65

Thus, in 3 out of 4 cases this coordination mechanism enables the dealing parties to achieve mutually beneficial trades; hence, at first glance, the mechanism appears rational and fair. But, because types are private information, the dealing parties may find it advantageous to lie about their real types.

Let w = weak, s = strong, and ws = weak who pretends to be strong. Hence,

for the seller:

$E(\Pi)w = (25 - 10)\,(1)(.5) + (65 - 10)(1)(.5) = 35;$

$E(\Pi)ws = 0 + (110 - 10)(1)(.5) = 50.$

Since 50 > 35, dishonesty would pay off for the seller;

for the buyer:

$E(\Pi)w = (120 - 110)(1)(.5) + (120 - 65)(1)(.5) = 32.5;$

$E(\Pi)ws = 0 + (120 - 25)(1)(.5) = 47.5.$

Since 47.5 > 32.5, dishonesty would pay off for the buyer.

Therefore, subject to split-the-difference mediation plan, both the buyer and the seller would have the incentive to be dishonest.

Coordination Mechanism Two: Symmetric Mediation plan

Consider now a different mediation plan as shown in Table 4. The cells, as above, contain probabilities and prices, where q is a conditional probability of trade applied to the respective cells; the conditional probability for (weak, weak) remains 1.

Table 4: Symmetric mediation plan

			Buyer's type & value	
			Strong (0.5)	Weak (0.5)
			\$40	\$120
Seller's type & value	Strong (0.5)	\$100	0, No trade	**q**, \$120-**y**
	Weak (0.5)	\$10	**q**, \$10+**y**	1, \$65

According to Myerson (2008, p. 591), "the probability of trade could also be interpreted as the conditional expected number of objects that the buyer would get in this case, and so $q \leq 1$ here can also be interpreted as a *resource constraint*, expressing the fact that there is only one object that they can trade; … for a strong trader to participate in this plan, y must satisfy the *participation constraint* y ≤ 20.” Thus, appropriate values of “q” and “y” will generate incentive compatibility. Proceeding as above,

for the seller:

$E(\Pi)w = (10 + y - 10)(q)(.5) + (65 - 10)(1)(.5)$

$E(\Pi)ws = (120 - y - 10)(q)(.5)$;

for honesty,

$E(\Pi)w \geq E(\Pi)ws$

or,

$q \leq 27.5/(55 - y)$;

for the buyer:

$E(\Pi)w = (120 - 120 + y)(q)(.5) + (120 - 65)(1)(.5)$

$E(\Pi)ws = 0 + (120 - 10 - y)(q)(.5)$;

for honesty,

$E(\Pi)w \geq E(\Pi)ws$

or,

$\mathbf{q \leq 27.5/(55 - y)}$.

Therefore, the incentive constraints $\mathbf{q \leq 27.5/(55 - y)}$ and $\mathbf{y \leq 20}$ can generate an infinite number of possible incentive compatible deals.

Factor 2 - Credibility

Deferment-type deals between entities may offer incentives for non-cooperation. A solution to this problem is to construct a deal that contains a credible commitment. According to Cooter and Ulen (1996, p.170), such a credible

> *commitment is achieved by foreclosing the opportunity to appropriate. The opportunity to appropriate is foreclosed by the high cost of liability (and) when the other party observes the foreclosing of an opportunity. ... To illustrate, Julius Caesar sometimes burned the bridges behind him as his army advanced on the enemy. Burning the bridges committed his army to attack by foreclosing the opportunity to retreat.*

Consider the following numerical example of a non-credible deal (one-shot game) between firms A and B:

B

A		Collaborate	Breach
	Invest	10, 10	-20, 20
	Don't Invest	0, 0	0, 0

A's strategies are "invest" and "don't invest". B's strategies are "collaborate" and "breach." Numbers in the cells correspond to A's payoffs (left) and B's payoffs (right) and both firms are aware of these numbers. Assume that B offers to collaborate to deliver a service or a product in exchange for an investment by A. Obviously, A does not have a dominant strategy: A would invest when B collaborates but when B breaches it would not. B's dominant strategy is "beach": it pays to breach no matter what A does. The Nash equilibrium is ("don't invest", "breach") which corresponds to the payoff of (0, 0).

Alternatively, the firms may consider a credible deal according to which A promises to invest and B, if it breaches, would pay A the amount of 30 for compensation. Subject to this deal, the matrix becomes:

		B	
		Collaborate	Breach
A	Invest	10, 10	10, -10
	Don't Invest	0, 0	0, 0

In this case, the dominant strategy for B is "collaborate" and for A "invest." The Nash equilibrium is ("invest", "collaborate") which corresponds to the payoff of (10, 10).

Credibility, in general, may be directly related to law enforceability (which pre-requires the signing of a formal contract and an effective as well as efficient legal infrastructure), and / or in case of a deal, the desire to build reputation, cultural similarities, and to favorable random occurrences (e.g., an unforeseen change of policy towards merging or an unexpected upturn of the economy conducive to investment and collaboration.)

Factor 3 – Multi-Period Deals

As it was stressed above, securing cooperation typically requires credible promises in one-shot deals. It is more likely though that a deal may involve an infinite horizon (for instance, when two entities merge forever or form a cartel) or a finite horizon (when the two entities know that their deal will end – for example, a deal between a lender and a borrower.) Such multi-period deals are governed by *discount factors* and *end of deal probabilities*.

Infinite-horizon deals

To identify some of the conditions that will sustain or break infinite-horizon deals consider the high price cartel game between A and B in the matrix below, where HP = high price and LP = low price:

B

		HP	LP
A	HP	60, 60	15, 95
	LP	87, 10	50, 50

If the deal is executed only once it has a Nash equilibrium at (LP, LP) and neither A nor B would have the incentive to adopt the (HP, HP) strategy; the strategy is not credible.

But if the deal can be executed an infinite number of times, A and B may agree to the following *trigger strategy* deal: *each one of us will charge the high price forever. If one of us breaches and charges the low price, the other player will 'discipline' the cheater by charging the low price in every period from then on.* Hence, cooperation implies "High Prices" whereas breaching implies "Low Prices."

As stated above, sometimes either breaching or cooperating may be optimal. Similarly, here, because the deal's life is infinite, a subset of discount factors may justify breaching, another subset may justify cooperation, and another subset may leave the parties uncertain.

Hence, if the deal lasts forever, A's Present Value (PV) from Cooperating and Breaching (where D = Discount Factor, $0 \leq D \leq 1$) are, respectively:

$PV^{A}_{Cooperating} = 60(1+D_A)/D_A$;

and,

$PV^{A}_{Breaching} = 37 + [50(1+D_A)/D_A]$.

Setting the respective PVs equal to each other and solving for D_A, firm A discovers the value of D_A that makes it indifferent between cooperating and breaching; this value is $D_A = 0.37$. Hence, when $D_A < 0.37$, A would prefer to cooperate; when $D_A > 0.37$, A would prefer to breach.

Similarly for B, the respective PV equations are:

$PV^{B}_{Cooperating} = 60(1+D_B)/D_B$; and,

$PV^{B}_{Breaching} = 45 + [50(1+D_B)/D_B]$.

The value of D_B at which B would be indifferent between cooperating and breaching is $D_B = 0.29$. Hence, B would prefer to cooperate when $D_B < 0.29$ and breach when $D_B > 0.29$.

Comparing the values of D (see line in Figure 4 below), when D_A and D_B are both lower than 0.29, A and B would have the incentive to cooperate in perpetuity; when D_A and D_B are both higher than 0.37, A and B would have no incentive to cooperate in perpetuity. When D_A and D_B are both between 0.29 and 0.37, the parties would be uncertain as to what to do; in this case, the utilization of additional criteria (that is, in addition to D) for the decision to cooperate or breach may remove some or all of the uncertainty.

Figure 4: The importance of the discount factor in an infinite horizon cartel

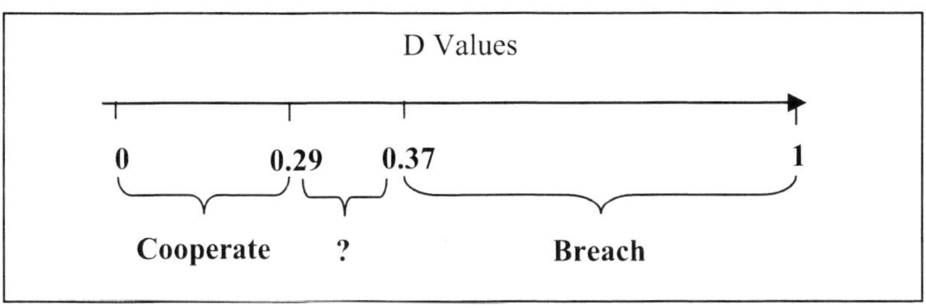

Deals with uncertain final periods

Because of abrupt changes in market environments the dealing parties may not know the precise date at which their products or services will become outmoded; in other words, they face uncertainty regarding the final period in which the deal will hold.

Suppose the probability that the deal will become useless after a given time period is Φ, where $O \leq \Phi \leq 1$. Without involving discounting, consider once more the payoffs in the infinite horizon deal example used above. For duopolist A, given its probability estimate Φ_A, the respective present values for cooperating or breaching would be:

$PV^A_{Cooperating} = 60/\Phi_A$; and,

$PV^A_{Breaching} = 37 + (50/\Phi_A)$.

Setting the respective PVs equal to each other and solving for Φ_A, A discovers the value of Φ_A at which it would be indifferent between cooperating and breaching; this value is $\Phi_A = 0.27$. If after each period the agreement survives, the probability that it will break-down is less than 27% percent, firm A will have the incentive to behave cooperatively; and if the same probability is greater than 27%, A would have the incentive to breach.

Similarly, for B, the respective PV equations are:

$PV^B_{Cooperating} = 60/\Phi_B$; and,

$PV^B_{Breaching} = 45 + (50/\Phi_B)$.

The value of Φ_B at which B would be indifferent between cooperating and breaching is $\Phi_B = 0.22$. Hence, B would prefer to cooperate when $\Phi_B < 0.22$ and breach when $\Phi_B > 0.22$.

Comparing the values of Φ (see line in Figure 5 below), when Φ_A and Φ_B are both lower than 0.22, A and B would have the incentive to stay in the deal for one more period; when Φ_A and Φ_B are both higher than 0.27, A and B would have the incentive to terminate the deal. When Φ_A and Φ_B are both between 0.22 and 0.27, the dealing parties would be even more uncertain as to what to do in the next period; in this case, the utilization of additional criteria (that is, in addition to Φ) for the decision to cooperate or breach may remove some or all of the uncertainty.

Figure 5: The importance of the final period in cartel agreements

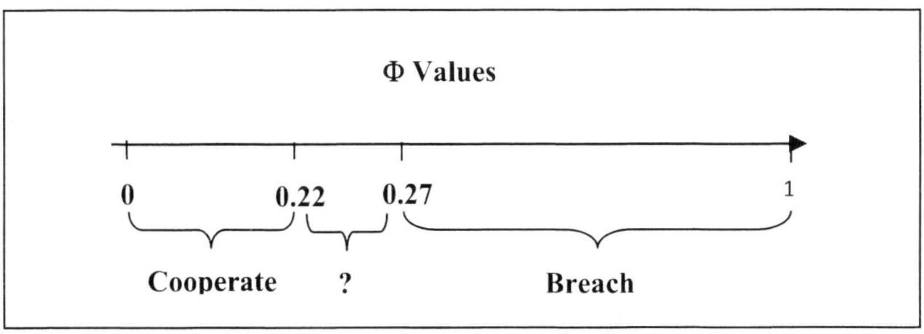

But, *what if the final period is known* to one of the contracting parties? If, for example, the deal is to last forever but entity A plans to terminate after six periods (let's say cooperate until the fifth and breach in the sixth) then there would be no tomorrow (no seventh period) during which B could instigate disciplinary action against A. In effect, then, because discipline is not possible during the last period, a party to an agreement has an incentive to break a promise in the second to the last time period. Because the firms know this, there is effectively no tomorrow in the third period from the last. This sort of "backward unscrambling" continues until the firms realize that no effective retribution can be used during any period. The cartel partners charge low prices in every period, right up to the known last period.

Given the payoffs in this example, A knows that B has the incentive to breach in the last period of the agreement no matter how many periods the agreement will last; similarly, for B. Therefore, if one of the firms knows its final period, then the other firm would have no incentive to hope for a 'tomorrow' in this cartel agreement. Due to mistrust, the deal would turn to a single-period, one-shot, bargain in which each entity would have the incentive to follow its dominating strategy of "low price" or "breaching" and hence realize a profit of $50 in the Nash equilibrium.[4]

Factor 4 - Optimal Commitments

As stressed in Section III above, a firm may manage its portfolio of promisor-type and promisee-type deals to minimize portfolio risk for a chance at higher expected profit. But how should the firm structure potential compensation remedies or damages? I attempt to answer this question with an example similar to the one used in Section III; the analysis and the example are modified versions of those offered by Cooter and Ulen (1996, p. 262).

A deal between entities X and Y may induce both to invest. If X is the promisor and Y the promisee, X may invest in performing and Y in reliance upon the promise. To illustrate, consider a deal between X (an air-shipping company) and Y (a pharmaceutical company in need of shipping, in timely fashion, of its new line of therapeutic medicine.) To fulfill the promise, X may have to invest, *in advance*, in airplanes conditioned to carry medicine cargo, which, currently, it does not possess. In anticipation of X's service, Y may invest, *in advance as well*, in additional and / or specific medicine producing capacity. Obviously, X and Y would be fully interdependent upon each other and the possibility of breaching would motivate them to consider possible compensation remedies with different incentive implications for investments in performance and reliance. At the end, in the deal, the promisor and the promisee should include optimal commitments to performance and reliance. Optimality, of course, requires accurate estimation of damages and it may involve third parties such as private arbitrators, courts or even government representatives.

Damages, paid by the promisor, may be computed on the basis of:

(1) Perfect Expectations. These damages leave the promisee *indifferent between performance and breach*.

(2) Perfect Reliance. These damages leave the promisee *indifferent between no deal and breach*.

(3) Perfect Opportunity-Cost. These damages leave the promisee *indifferent between breach and performance of the best alternative deal.* (Similarly for damages paid by the promisee.)

For example, consider the pharmaceutical firm used for illustration above in conjunction with the following possible linear functional relationship, representing a perfect substitutability iso-utility curve between M and S where M = dollar value of damages in millions, and S = service as a percent;

$$M = 50 - bS, \quad 0 \leq S \leq 1.$$

Consider Figure 6 which portrays three such indifference curves:

$M = 50 - (50/1)S$, for perfect expectations (E) with $0 \leq S \leq 1$,

$M = 50 - (50/0.5)S$, for perfect reliance (R) with $0 \leq S \leq 0.5$, and

$M = 50 - (50/0.75)S$, for perfect opportunity cost (OC) with $0 \leq S \leq 0.75$.

The air-shipping firm may deliver service ranging from totally inadequate (0%) to perfect (100%). Damages may be computed subject to three indifference curves. First, assume that the deal between X and Y requires perfect expectations damages, in other words the possibilities associated with curve E. If the air-shipper delivers 100% perfect service, the pharmaceutical firm would be happy and have no reason to file for remuneration. But, if, at the end, the service is only 25%, the pharmaceutical firm would be equally satisfied only if, in addition, it receives a $37.50 million compensation for damages.

Figure 6: Damages based on expectations, reliance and opportunity

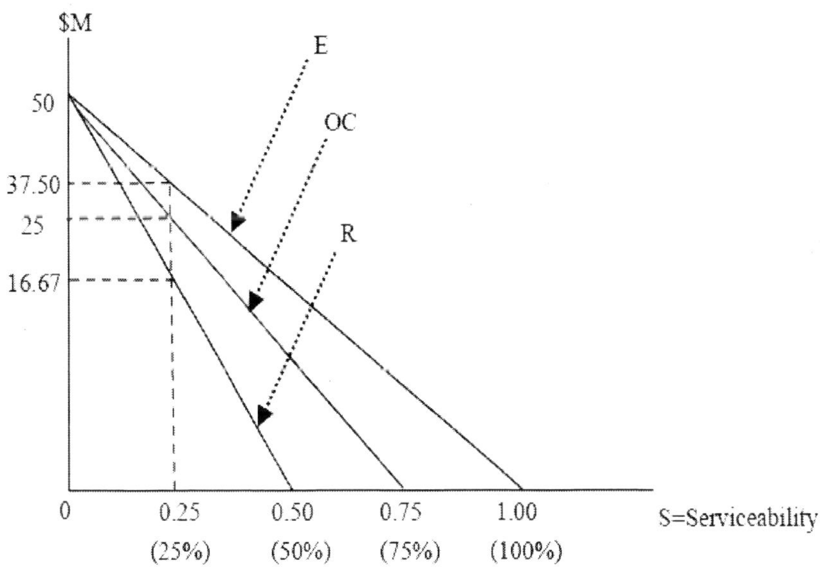

Second, assume that, prior to the deal, the pharmaceutical's own serviceability (by relying on its own efforts for delivery) is 50% and that the deal between X and Y requires perfect reliance damages, or the possibilities associated with curve R. If the air-shipper delivers 50% service (as it used to be the case prior to the deal), the pharmaceutical firm would be content and have no reason to request remuneration. But, if, at the end, the service is only 25%, the pharmaceutical firm would be equally content only if, in addition, it receives a $25 million compensation for damages.

Third, assume that the pharmaceutical firm, instead, could have hired a competing air-shipping firm which would have achieved 75% of the needed service. In this case, the deal between Y and X requires that if X does not deliver at least 75% service, Y is entitled to remuneration. In this case, the deal between X and Y requires perfect opportunity-cost damages, or the possibilities associated with curve OC. If the air-shipper delivers 75% service (as the competing firm would have delivered prior to the deal), the pharmaceutical firm would be satisfied and have no reason to demand remuneration. But, if, at the end, the service is only 25%, the pharmaceutical firm would be equally content only if, in addition, it receives a $16.67 million compensation for damages.

In addition to the above compensation schemes, the dealing parties may consider, among other: (a) *restitution* (it requires that the promisee receives back what it gave to a breaching promisor for the deal – for example, a down payment;) and (b) *disgorgement* (compensation received by the promisee equal to the profit made by the promisor for misconduct – for example, promisor X promises to deliver a service to promisee Y but instead it delivers the service to someone else.)

Factor 5 – Efficient Default Terms

Undoubtedly, deals may be affected by unexpected events such as natural disasters, wars, strikes, etc. For example, in the above builder / hospital example, how would the builder deal with the promise to deliver when a construction workers' strike breaks out? Similarly, how would the hospital keep its side of the promise when an unexpected malpractice lawsuit against it drives the entity to bankruptcy before the completion of the building? Deals, unfortunately, suffer from gaps (events not unambiguously addressed in the deal that have an effect on commitments created by it.) Such gaps may be unintentional (due to inability to foresee future contingencies) or intentional (due to attaching low probabilities of future contingencies occurring.) Entities expect to save transaction costs by intentionally leaving gaps in deals whenever the actual cost of negotiating explicit terms exceeds the expected cost of filling a gap. For example, in the above builder / hospital example, the entities may experience, ex ante, \$1000 in transaction costs (negotiations, time delays, etc.) on whether or not to include in their deal provisions for the contingency of a strike. Alternatively, they may leave a gap in the deal by choosing to ignore the strike contingency. Let's assume that the strike happens and, ex post, the parties incur \$20000 in losses inclusive of transaction costs. What should the dealing parties do, depends on the probability of strike:

Ex Ante Cost = (Ex Post Cost)(P), where P =probability of strike,

or

\$1000 = (\$20000)(P).

If $P = 0.05$, the parties would be indifferent between allocating costs before or after. If $P < 0.05$, it pays to leave a gap in the deal. If $P > 0.05$, it pays to fill the gap.

Of course, in the real world, the task of filling gaps in deals may be influenced by third parties most likely courts and semi-governmental or governmental institutions (for example, the local or international Chamber of Commerce or the Commerce Departments of various nations.) In general, in the absence of unambiguous terms to the contrary, implicit terms would fill gaps by default. If default terms were efficient, then deals with gaps would make more sense than deals with filled gaps. But, what does efficiency entail? Once more, this question may be answered with the assistance of the builder / hospital example. Suppose the two parties leave the gap about the strike in their deal and the builder can bear the risk of the strike at a cost of $800 while the hospital can bear the risk at $3000. In this case, if the default rule shifts risk to the party that can bear it at a lower cost (the builder) the parties, in total, will save $3000 - $800 = $2200 which constitutes an improvement in efficiency.

Factor 6 - Repair Malfunctions by Regulating the Conditions of Deals

Agents often are unable to continue performing due to reasons beyond their control (e.g, accidents, disease, coercion, etc.), the harmful influence of third parties, bad information (deception, non-disclosing of history, different misinformation or monopoly / monopsony exploitation. Such malfunctions may be repaired through bilateral and flexible regulations of the conditions of deals.

(a) Malfunction may be due to the inability of the dealing parties to continue as rational agents (or continue having stable preferences.) For example, dealing parties may become ***inept*** due to accidents, disease or other factors and as a result they may not be able to carry a deal to the end; in this case, deals have to be modified subject to the involvement of a private professional arbitrator (for example auditor), the justice system or the government. Similarly, if one of the parties has to carry on with a deal subject to ***coercion*** (imposed, usually, by the promisee) or to ***desperation*** (caused, usually, by the promisor) such an opportunistic deal would be unethical and, legally, unenforceable. Likewise, if unlikely events (for example, acts of God, wars, civil unrest) thwart performance, then deals may become ***impossible beyond reasonable control*** to carry through.

(b) Additionally, malfunction may be a function of ***third party effects***. A third party, other than the promisor or promisee, may intervene and cause the breakup of a deal when the deal derogates public policy. For example, if according to public policy industrial pollution is unacceptable, and a deal between industrialists A and B causes environmental degradation, a third party – such as Citizens United Against Pollution – may bring about a break up in the deal through the court system, government or other means. On the other hand, if one of the dealing parties purposely brings in a third party to blackmail the other, such conduct would violate the unwritten obligation to deal in good faith. For illustration, consider, again, the builder / hospital example: the builder has agreed to deliver at a certain price; in the middle of construction though, for good reason, the builder attempts to renegotiate a higher price by threatening to stop operations and instead offer its construction services to a third party who would pay less. The builder's deal with the third party frustrates negotiating with the hospital; it ties up the hands of both; it contributes to the belittlement of a legal obligation which makes the deal between the builder and the third party unenforceable.

(c) Moreover, promise-breaching may be accepted on the ground that the promise was made subject to bad information such as:

Deception or lack of warning. For illustration, in the builder / hospital example, the builder must not misinform the hospital about the building's capability to sustain an earthquake, even though after revealing the truth the deal may not go through.

Non-disclosing the history of faults upon request or not-satisfying an implied performance warranty. When a firm purchases *used equipment* from another, the seller, at the buyer's request, must truthfully make available the history of the equipment; for example, the buyer may ask whether or not the equipment was ever in a flood or in a fire, whether or not it was regularly serviced, and so forth. Or, when a firm purchase *new equipment* from another, the buyer is entitled to an implied warranty of fitness according to which the equipment is appropriate to use for its intended purpose; for example, when a tracking firm buys a track for transportation of goods, the implied warranty does not apply when the buyer uses the track for the transportation of people.

Frustration of Purpose. The problem occurs when dealing entities base the deal upon the *same* misinformation. For illustration, in the builder/hospital example, both entities expect an increase of population in the vicinity of the hospital because of incoming immigration; but because of unexpected events the influx of immigrants is delayed leaving the hospital with less revenue than expected to fulfill its deal with the builder. Hence, the change in circumstances frustrates the purpose of the deal between the two parties and the courts or other institutions would be reluctant to enforce.

Mutual Mistake. Alternatively, parties may draft deals based on different misinformation. For example, firm A sells two kinds of large internal combustion engines: one burning gasoline, the other diesel. B strikes a deal with A to purchase an engine. A, truthfully believing that B has ordered the gasoline engine, proceeds with the shipment of that engine. Upon arrival, B expresses its disappointment truthfully believing that it negotiated to receive the diesel engine. Hence, like with frustration of purpose, the deal between the two parties cannot stand and the courts or other institutions would be reluctant to enforce. Instead, they may ask A to return the money and B to return the engine.

Monopoly and Monopsony. When the party to involve in a deal is the only available party, a deal is exposed to possible monopolistic or monopsonistic exploitation which may be eased with the involvement of the court system, government or other institutions. The court system for example may rely on the doctrine of *unconscionability* according to which a deal is unfair when its enforcement violates the conscience of the court. For illustration, if the hospital operates in a competitive market (a competitive firm) and it signs a deal with the only builder in the region (a monopoly firm) to supply its construction needs for the next 50 years but the builder can drop the hospital at any time for other clients, the deal is not fair; the time horizon for the hospital is 50 years but for the builder the time horizon is any number of years. According to this deal, the hospital cannot drop the builder for a competing builder prior to the 50th year. In this case, if the hospital wants to break away from the agreement, let's say in the 4th year, and the builder refuses to accept, the deal would be viewed as too uneven to carry legal strength and a court may rule in favor of the hospital on the ground of unconscionability.

Factor 7 – Satisfy Offer, Acceptance, Consideration and Meeting of Minds

The principles of offer, acceptance and consideration, subject to meeting of minds, have to be satisfied for a deal between two firms. Consider firms X and Y; X may "offer" a service to Y and, in turn, Y may respond with "acceptance". "Consideration" is what X (Y) gives up or does which is either to its detriment or to Y's (X's) benefit.

Consider some examples: Let X be an information technology (IT) firm and Y an accounting firm. X offers to Y computer maintenance services to take place in the first week of December.

Case 1: Y accepts and pays a non-returnable deposit to X in advance of the IT services. The IT services, in the minds of both, entail removal of viruses and other such malicious files unwillingly downloaded through internet browsing. When the time arrives X informs Y that she would not be able to offer the promised IT services. Y may file a lawsuit against X for breaching the contract because the principles of "offer", "acceptance", "consideration" (deposit paid) as well as "meeting of minds" are all satisfied.

Case 2: Y accepts. The IT services, in the minds of both, entail removal of viruses and other such malicious files unwillingly downloaded through internet browsing. When the time arrives X informs Y that she would not be able to offer the promised IT services. In this case, although the principles of "offer", "acceptance", and "meeting of minds" are all satisfied "consideration" is not (no deposit exchanged hands or anything else occurred that benefited X to the detriment of Y.) Therefore, Y may not file a lawsuit against X for breaching the contract.

Case 3: Y accepts and pays a non-returnable deposit to X in advance of the IT services. The IT services, in the mind of Y, entails removal of viruses and other such malicious files unwillingly downloaded through internet browsing; but, in the mind of X, IT services implies dusting off Y's computers. When the time arrives Y is unpleasantly surprised to realize exactly what X means by IT services. In this case, although the principles of "offer", "acceptance", and "consideration" are all satisfied "meeting of minds" is not. Therefore, Y may not file a lawsuit against X for breaching the contract.

V. Summary & Conclusion

Incomplete information, global markets, reputation and even behavioral issues complicate contract writing to say the least, making management of deals a business function of paramount importance. I define *deal* as a reciprocal duty subject to incentives, reputation, ethics, cultural norms, circumstances, and essential legal elements. Deals may be more effective than ordinary contracts in today's global environment characterized by, traditional firms, service firms, knowledge firms, escalating complexity and rising international competition. Because of the variety and complexity of hybrid forms the firm may be viewed as a function of deals instead of contracts. Deals encompass a wider range of contingencies and as such they may evolve more efficiently, effectively and flexibly.

Deals, like traditional contracts, are about intra- and inter-group, more or less specific relationships that aim to contribute to a firm more than the firm could gain on its own. Deals differ from traditional contracts in that they are more adaptation-intensive, less change resisting; they establish a framework (written or unwritten) within which firms may move more freely in their quest for information to lessen uncertainty and asymmetry and to more successfully cope with change and competition (e.g., breaching under a deal may be less costly than under a traditional contract). As the business / economics environment optimizes and as it naturally selects business blueprints suitable to the environment that firms operate in, it simultaneously selects the deals that govern relationships between firms. Deals that are naturally selected are fit for survival, they need less policing, are less prone to opportunism and are subject to lower costs.

In the paragraphs above, I attempted to offer a justification as to why the profit-making firm may be viewed as a function of its nucleus expertise and a risky portfolio of deals between it and any internal as well as external agents. More specifically, it was argued that in addition to gaining from competitive advantage, the firm can gain even more if it reduces the riskiness of its portfolio of promisor-type and promisee-type deals. In its effort to reduce such risk, the firm needs to know each deal's profit share and be able to estimate each dealing partner's reliability (a random variable). It was stressed that, for effective and efficient management of a portfolio of deals, the firm needs to take into consideration factors such as, among other: mediation; credibility; multi-period deals; optimal commitments; efficient default terms; repair malfunctions by regulating the conditions of deals; offer, acceptance, consideration and meeting of minds.

Endnotes

1. A similar deal is discussed below in the section titled Optimal Commitments.

2. Optimum profit shares for minimum risk may easily be found via calculus; see Kantarelis (2010, Chapter 6).

3. As defined by American Arbitration Association, the American Bar Association and the Society of Professionals in Dispute Resolution (Canadian Foundation for Dispute Resolution, 2012),

> *mediation is a process in which an impartial third party -- a mediator -- facilitates the resolution of a dispute by promoting voluntary agreement (or "self-determination") by the parties to the dispute. A mediator facilitates communications, promotes understanding, focuses the parties on their interests, and seeks creative problem solving to enable the parties to reach their own agreement. These standards give meaning to this definition of mediation.*

4. The deals considered above are games with pure strategies, they involve simultaneous play, and they are one-shot or multi-period. For additional games, namely, games with mixed strategies, incomplete games, and evolutionary games see Kantarelis (2010)

and various texts on game theory. Additionally, many other essential elements are missing: the PV computation does not include the inflation rate or discount factors or payoffs that vary through time.

References

Beuve, J and S. Saussier, (2012), "Interfirm cooperation in strategic relationships: the role of formal contract", Industrial and Corporate Change, Volume 21, Issue 4, pp 811-836.

Canadian Foundation for Dispute Resolution (CFDR), (2012), < http://www.cfdr.org/med_proc4.htm>)

Coase, R., (1937), "The Nature of the Firm", Economica , Vol. 4, pp 386-405.

Cooter, R. and Ulen, T., (1996), Law and Economics, 2nd ed, Addison-Wesley.

Hayek, Friedrich A., (1945), 'The Use of Knowledge in Society', American Economic Review, Vol XXXV, #4, pp. 519-30.

Kantarelis, Demetri, (2003), "Building Blocks for an Evolutionary Theory of the Firm: Review & Analysis", Journal of Business & Public Affairs, August.

Kantarelis, Demetri, (2010), Theories of the Firm, 3rd ed., Inderscience.

Kim, J. and J. T. Mahoney, (2010), "A Strategic Theory of the Firm as a Nexus of Incomplete Contracts: A Property Rights Approach", Journal of Management, Volume 36, Issue 4, pp 806-826.

Lintner, John, (1965), "The Valuation of Risk Assets and the Selection of Risky Investments in Stock Portfolios and Capital Budgets," Review of Economics and Statistics 47,1: 13-37.

Markowitz, Harry, (1959), Portfolio Selection: Efficient Diversifications of Investments, Cowels Foundation Monograph No 16, John Wiley.

Masten, Scott E. (Editor), (1996), Case Studies in Contracting and Organization, Oxford University Press.

Myerson, Roger B., (2008), 'Perspectives on Mechanism Design in Economic Theory', American Economic Review, Vol 98, #3, pp 586-603.

O'Reilly III, C. A. and B. G. M. Main, (2010), "Economic and psychological perspectives on CEO compensation: a review and synthesis", Industrial and Corporate Change, Volume 19, Issue 3, pp 675-712.

Rendon, Rene G., (2006). "Measuring Contract Management Process Maturity: A Tool for Enhancing the Value Chain", U.S.

Naval Postgraduate School, 91st Annual International Supply Management Conference. <http://www.ism.ws/files/pubs/proceedings/acrendon.pdf>

Reve, Torger, (1990), "The Firm as a nexus of Internal and External Contracts," The Firm as a Nexus of Treaties, M. Aoki, B. Gustafsson and O. Williamson, ed., Sage.

Sgourev, S. V. and Ezra W. Zuckerman, (2011), "Breaking up is hard to do: Irrational inconsistency in commitment to an industry peer network", Rationality and Society, 23 no. 1, pp 3-34.

Treynor, J.L., (1962), "Towards a Theory of Market Value of Risky Assets," in Asset Pricing and Portfolio Performance, 1999, Robert A. Korjczyk, ed., Risk Books: 15-22.

Williamson, O, (1985), The Economic Institutions of Capitalism, Free Press.

Yunus, Muhammad (Peace Nobel Laureate 2006) <http://www.nobelprize.org/nobel_prizes/peace/laureates/2006/>

Chapter 3:

Contracts & Banking

I. Introduction

Without a doubt, the great global recession of the 2007 / 2008 may be called a banking crisis since it was mostly triggered by the failure of banks to manage risk. More specifically, many pre-crisis banks violated basic banking contractual principles contributing to high default rates and the drainage of default insurance funds. As the tumultuous year of 2008 was coming to its end, the realization over what transpired came into focus: (a) from 2003 on capital inflow had been flooding US markets; this capital, in search of high returns in well-developed capital markets, was coming from countries with developing or weak capital markets, mostly made from the sale of commodities such as oil (Russia and Saudi Arabia among other) and / or manufacturing goods (China and India among other). (b) In search of assets, the capital inflow, along with easy monetary policy, fueled real estate markets feeding sub-prime lending, the derivatives / securitization frenzy and of course defaults, faulty bond rating, bank failures and massive bail outs.

My objective in this chapter is to describe a simple bank firm model, discuss the main theoretical lessons derived from it and then contrast the lessons against the great global financial crisis. In sections II-V, I describe a conventional, representative, model about an integrated firm, which simultaneously sells assets and lends money to asset buyers (homogeneous or heterogeneous in terms of risk-type), and discuss a range of theoretical principles (primarily lessons on how to minimize adverse selection and moral hazard in lending.) In sections VI-VII, I make an attempt to contrast the model's principles against the global financial crisis especially as it relates to sub-prime lending in the USA.

II. A Theory of the Banking Firm

Adams, Einav and Levin (2009) and, preceding them, Jaffee and Russell (1976), have proposed and utilized a simple theoretical model to show how various credit constraints may minimize problems associated with adverse selection and moral hazard in the principal-agent relationship between a bank and its clients. In the following sections I present a similar model, enriched with more details, which consists of the following simplifying assumptions and functional relationships:

(a) There are a large number of competing integrated firms (e.g., a bank owns real estate for which it offers loans.)

(b) There are a large number of homogeneous clients. Clients are all the same type (there is no differentiation between high and low risk types.)

(c) Two periods. In the first period, a client decides on the size of a loan to purchase an asset (e.g. house); in the second period the client decides whether to pay back her loan.

(d) Contract. The representative bank offers a contract specifying a down payment (D) equal to the price of the asset (P) minus the amount of the loan (L), to be paid by the client in the first period, and a second period loan liability (M) equal to the contractual interest rate (R) times the loan, to be paid by the client in the second period. Hence, the first period contractual obligation is

$$D = P - L$$

while the second period contractual obligation is

$$M = RL.$$

(e) Probability of repayment. The probability of repayment (P_R) is assumed to be a negative function of loan liability M, or

$$P_R = f(M),\ f_M < 0. \qquad (1)$$

This default assumption is plausible because of circumstances (in the second period the client's income may unexpectedly decrease and/or the market value of the asset may decrease below the loan liability) or moral hazard caused by individual decisions. According to Adams, Einav and Levin (p. 66), "the equilibrium predictions of the model, and its ability to explain credit limits, simply do not depend on the specific breakdown" as to why the client defaults.

(f) Expected utility. Let U = expected utility expressed as a function of D and M, decreasing in both variables, or

$$U = U(D, M),\quad U_D < 0 \quad \text{and} \quad U_M < 0. \qquad (2)$$

An iso-expected utility curve $U_* = U(D, M)$ (where U_* = given U), derived from (2), is graphed in Figure 1.

Figure 1: Iso-expected utility curve

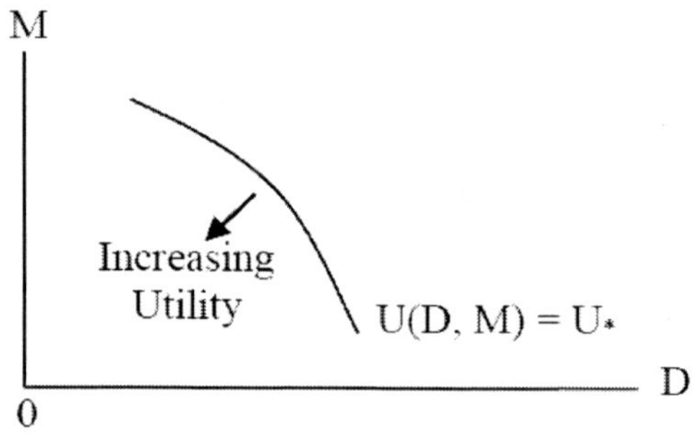

(g) Expected profit. Let Π = expected profit expressed as a function of D and M. Function (3) is increasing in D because with fixed M, a higher D would be to the bank's advantage. However, because of function (1), expected profit increases with M up to a certain point and thereafter it declines.

$$\Pi = \Pi\,(D, M), \tag{3}$$

$\Pi_D > 0$ and up to a point $\Pi_M > 0$ thereafter $\Pi_M < 0$.

An iso-expected profit curve $\Pi_* = \Pi(D, M)$ (where Π_* = given Π), derived from (3), is graphed in Figure 2.

Figure 2: Iso-expected profit curve

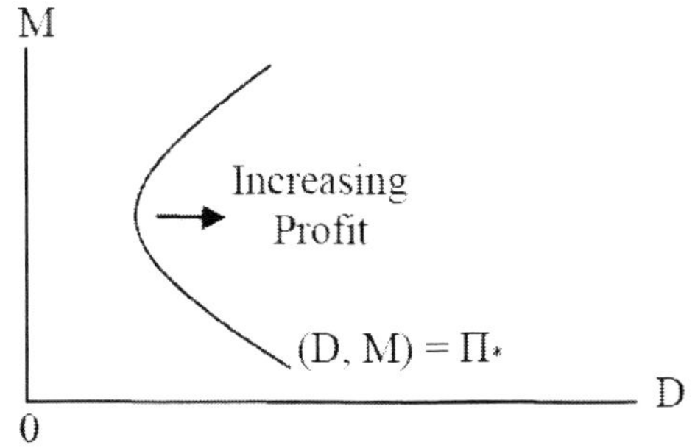

III. Loan limits and moral hazard

Suppose a client purchases an asset at price P on a loan L. If she defaults then M = 0 and the bank will acquire the asset at C, where C = cost of acquiring the asset. Hence, Π(C, 0) is one of the possible points on Π(D, M) = 0, the bank's zero iso-expected profit curve, displayed in Figure 3 as Π_0. Clearly, the bank would not accept a down payment less than D_l or, given $P \geq C$, offer a loan greater than $(P - D_l)$. Undoubtedly, this loan limit protects the bank against moral hazard.

Figure 3: Zero iso-expected profit curve

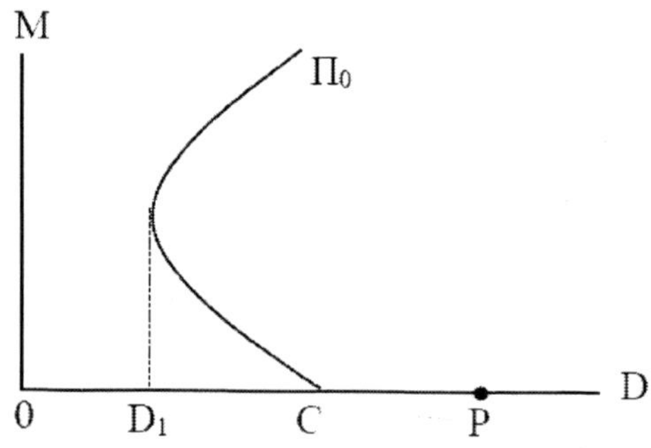

IV. Equilibrium

As shown in Figure 4, equilibrium occurs at e, the point of tangency between the iso-expected profit curve (Π_0) and the iso-expected utility curve (U_*). Since M = RL, the bank can offer the following two contracts at e:

Contract I:

L_1 with down payment D_e and interest rate $R_1 = M_e / L_1$

or,

Contract II:

L_2 with down payment D_e and interest rate $R_2 = M_e / L_2$

Obviously, $R_1 > R_2$ (line eP_1 is steeper than line eP_2.) In other words, contract II implies that the integrated firm (bank and seller of asset) can charge a higher price for the asset, require a higher

Figure 4: Equilibrium

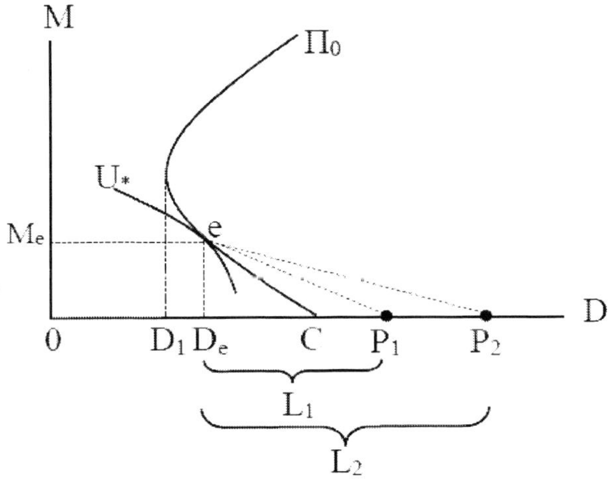

down payment than D_1 and offer a larger loan at a lower interest rate. Thus, the bank would not offer loans greater than the difference between the price of the asset and the equilibrium down payment; if it does, it would incur losses.

V. Heterogeneous clients and adverse selection

Borrowers, of course, are not homogeneous; some are high-risk types and other low-risk types. Graphically, as shown in Figure 5, high-risk types are those with steeper iso-expected utility curves.

Figure 5: High-risk type vs. low-risk type borrower

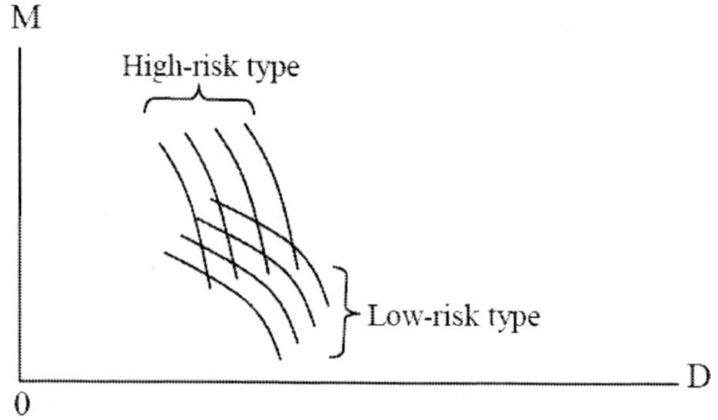

If the bank knows the type of the its borrower, given that the same asset price is paid by both types, it will require that, relative to the low-risk type, the high-risk type pays a higher interest rate, comes up with a higher deposit and applies for a smaller loan. Figure 6 displays zero iso-expected profit curves for high-risk (Π_H) and low-risk (Π_L) types as well as iso-expected utility curves for high-risk (U_{1H}) and low-risk (U_{1L}) borrowers. For the low-risk type at equilibrium (1_L), down payment and interest rate are lower while loan size is greater than for the high-risk type at equilibrium (1_H).

Of course, if, due to lack of information, the bank cannot distinguish between risk types, it may rely on an average iso-expected profit curve, such as Π_A in Figure 5, to set lending parameters. Obviously, with Π_A, the bank will experience adverse selection: the high-risk type borrower will end up improving her utility (from U_{1H} to U_{2H}) by paying a lower down payment for a larger loan at equilibrium 2_H relative to the low-risk type at equilibrium 2_L whose utility declines from U_{1L} to U_{2L}.

Figure 6: High-risk vs. low-risk borrowers and adverse selection

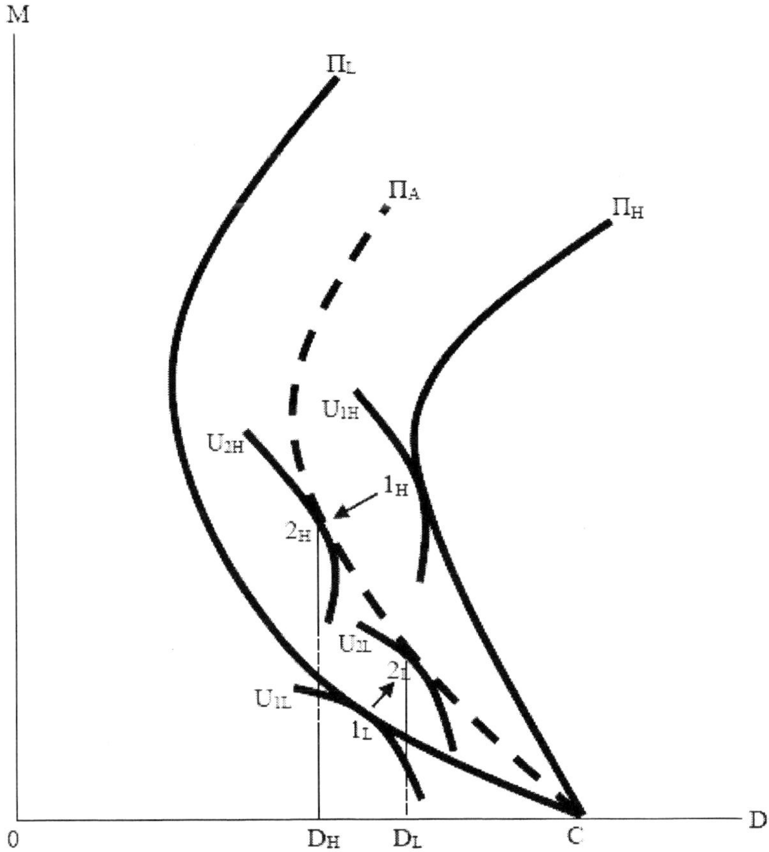

VI. Theory versus reality

The theoretical lessons for the representative bank, drawn from the model under consideration, are as follows:

1. Distinguish between high / low risk clients;
2. Charge higher (lower) interest rates for high (low) risk clients.
3. Require a higher (lower) down payment for high (low) risk clients;
4. Limit the down payment so that $\Pi(D, M) \geq 0$.

Unfortunately, during the 2007-08 financial crisis we found out that many banks in the USA had not learned these lessons. As reported by Mayer, Pence and Sherlund (p. 27), according to the Mortgage Bankers Association, the share of seriously delinquent loans increased from 0.7% in 1979 to 5.2% in 2008, followed by a 62% increase in foreclosures from 1.1 million in 2007 to 1.7 million in 2008 (Table 1, first two columns).

As explained by Mayer, Pence and Sherlund (p. 27) "defaults of mortgage loans are particularly concentrated among borrowers whose mortgages are classified as … non-prime" (where non-prime is the sum of sub-prime and near-prime.)

Table 1(last column) contains the sub-prime and near-prime total loans indicating that, from 2003 to 2005, sub-prime loans increased about 73% whereas near-prime soared about 267%.

Thereafter, both categories of loans started to decline dropping to zero in 2008.

Table 1: Seriously delinquent loans and foreclosures

Year	Share of seriously delinquent loans	Foreclosures (millions)	Total Non-prime loans (millions)
1979	0.7 %		
2003			1.1 SP, 0.3 NP (10% share of all mortgages)
2005			1.9 SP, 1.1 NP (32 % share of all mortgages)
2007 (I-III)		1.1	
2008 (III)	5.2 %		
2008 (I-III)		1.7	

Source of data and definitions: Mayer, Pence and Sherlund (pp. 27-29)

SP = sub-prime (loans targeted to borrowers who have tarnished credit histories and little savings available for down payments.)

NP = near-prime (loan targeted to borrowers with more minor credit quality issues or borrowers who are unable or unwilling to provide full documentation of assets or income; some of these borrowers are investing in real estate rather than occupying the properties they purchase. Near-prime mortgages are often bundled into securities.)

Mayer, Pence and Sherlund (pp. 28-30) report that they found little evidence to support the notion that delinquencies were related to non-prime loans; instead, their evidence points-out that the most damaging factors were originate-to-distribute loans, interest rates, and house prices. As they put it, according to the originate-to-distribute model

> *mortgage brokers originated loans and then sold them to institutions that securitized them. (75% of sub-prime*

> *originations were securitized in recent years.) As brokers did not bear the ultimate costs of default, they may have had a lower incentive to screen applicants carefully. We find that underwriting deteriorated along several dimensions: more loans were originated to borrowers with very small down payments and little or no documentation of their income or assets, in particular. ...We find substantial evidence that declines in house prices are a key factor in the current problems facing the mortgage market.*

Although sub-prime borrowers were riskier than near-prime borrowers the originate-to-distribute model, within each risk pool, removed the incentive of the lender to search for and discriminate against high-risk types. Additionally, this opportunistic model gave incentives to originating lenders for manipulation and inflation of appraisals of homes purchased as either goods or assets. Moreover, it falsely raised the hopes of borrowers, encouraging them to discount the long-term costs of loans, and it contributed to the profits of lenders since it was advantageous to them not to detect such errors.

Obviously, the originate-to-distribute lending practitioners did not really take into consideration any of the lessons derived from the theoretical analysis of the representative bank model discussed above.

VII. The global financial crisis

Although, undoubtedly, the impact of the "originate-to-distribute" factor on the global financial crisis was harmful, it not only caused problems; other factors in the toxic environment caused it as well. Such factors (among other) were:

(a) **Deregulation**. It has been documented that the practice of non-prime lending, which gave rise to originate-to-distribute loans, started in the 1990s during the Clinton administration for the purpose of financial capital democratization and continued during the Bush administration. As reported by Mayer, Pence and Sherlund (p. 28), "a Department of Housing and Urban Development report published in 2000 documented 'the rapid growth of sub-prime lending during the 1990s' and called for increased scrutiny of sub-prime lending due to 'growing evidence of widespread predatory practices in the sub-prime market.' Despite these concerns, lending to risky borrowers grew rapidly in the 2000s." (See Table 1.)

(b) **Securitization**. Originate-to-distribute loans without effective regulation, or incentive-efficient mechanisms, failed to produce good risks; instead, they generated an environment conducive to adverse selection totally dry of incentive-compatibility. The buying bank of the originate-to-distribute loans securitized bad-risk along with good-risk mortgages accompanied by false rating and non-adequately collateralized default insurance.

As explained by Ramady & Kantarelis (2009, p.327), such default insurance contracts, known as "credit default swaps" (CDS), were offered mostly by American International Group (AIG) on packages of debt known as "collateralized debt obligations" (CDO) - pools of loans sliced into tranches and sold to investors based on the credit quality of the underlying securities. (Unfortunately, rating firms, although good in rating single entities, they were not very good in rating multi-entity tranches.) Believing that it would never have to pay claims, the immensely reputable and highly rated AIG decided to start selling CDS contracts at very low premiums for a four or five-year horizon, to any CDO holder that would knock on their door. Although, the low premiums were a bargain for good risks they were also a bargain for bad risks, causing AIG to adversely select its contracts.

(c) **Easy monetary policy.** According to O'Driscoll Jr. (2009), the trigger was easy monetary policy. O'Driscoll Jr. (p.4), quotes Anna Schwartz who said, "the basic propagator was too-easy monetary policy and too-low interest rates" and states that, O'Driscoll Jr. (p.4),

> *in the housing boom, easy money and cheap credit financed an unsustainable increase in investment in residential real estate. Especially in the hottest real estate markets, buying took on a frenzied aspect. ... (and according to John Taylor) the Fed pushed short-term interest rates below levels predicted by an economic model of monetary policy based on historical patterns.*

(d) **Inflow of capital**. During the 2000s, commodity-selling nations (China, India, oil producing countries and other), with not very well developed domestic capital markets, decided to invest their newly accumulated wealth in various well developed capital markets around the world, mostly in the USA. The resulted capital inflow flooded US capital markets and contributed to excess demand for assets, especially real estate assets, via originate-to-distribute practices. According to Caballero, Farhi and Pierre-Gourinchas (2008, pp. 7-8),

> *Emerging markets and commodity producers found themselves more than ever in search of investment opportunities. In effect, U.S. assets became stretched by trying to accommodate the world's excess demand for assets ... (derived) ... from financial underdevelopment in emerging markets and most commodity-producing economies, rather from macroeconomic imbalances. ... Excess asset demand leaves an unmistakable signature in low*

real interest rates, which in turn provide a fertile ground for bubbles to emerge.

Flow Chart 1: Vicious cycles (financial crisis: 2005-09)

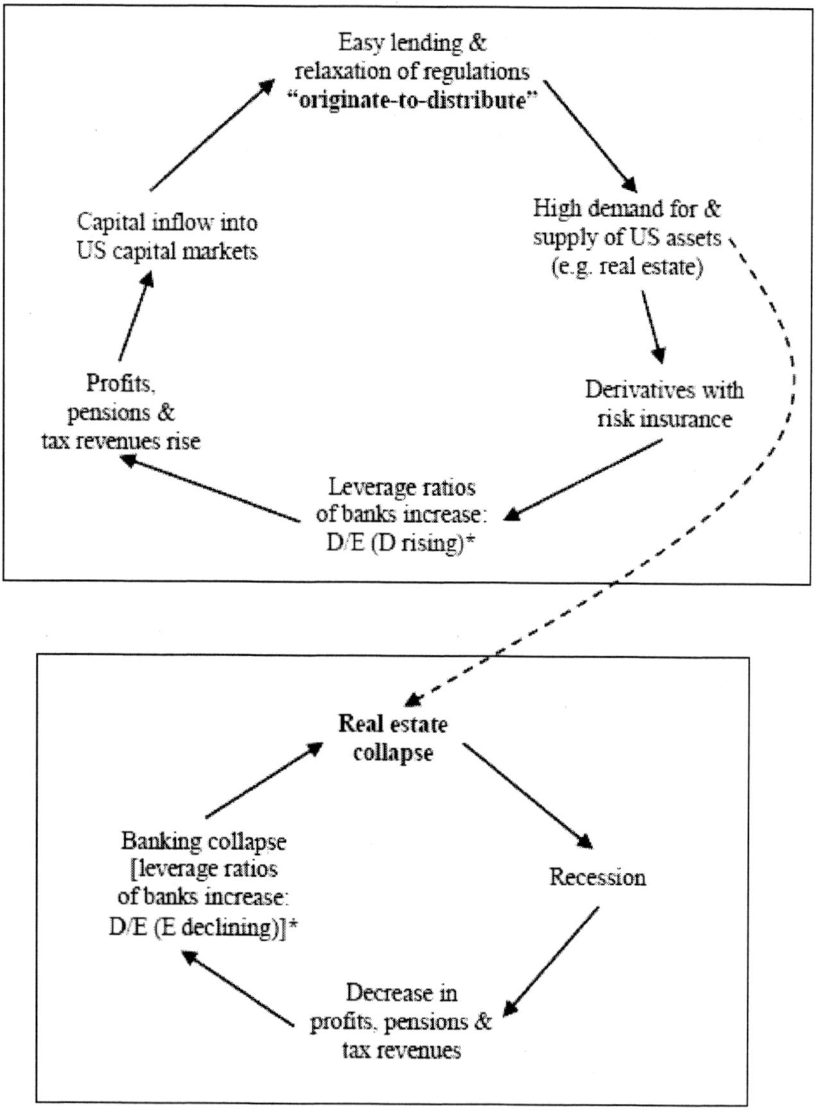

* D=debt, E=equity.

In other words, the increase in oil and other commodity prices, the unusually large international capital inflows into the well-developed US capital markets, the easy monetary policy, the harmful practice of "originate-to-distribute" loans, and other factors, triggered the vicious cycle (circular causation) in the upper box of Flow Chart 1. In turn, the real estate market triggered the vicious cycle in the lower box, which, to this day, has not stopped spinning.

VIII. Summary & Conclusion

In this chapter I described a conventional, representative, model about an integrated firm, which simultaneously sells assets and lends money to asset buyers (homogeneous or heterogeneous in terms of risk-type), and discussed various theoretical principles (lessons) that may guide lenders in their effort to minimize adverse selection and moral hazard in lending. These lessons stress the importance of down payment, loan size, loan liability and other information (e.g., credit history) that enables lenders to discriminate between low-risk and high-risk borrowers.

In turn, I made an attempt to contrast the model's principles against the recent financial crisis especially as it relates to sub-prime lending in the USA. The main conclusion is that the model's theoretical principles were violated. More specifically, the unusually large international capital inflows into US capital markets, the easy monetary policy, the harmful practice of "originate-to-distribute" loans along with securitization based on faulty ratings, and the anti-regulation efforts of past governments to promote financial capital democratization, blocked lenders' efforts (took away incentives) to minimize adverse selection and moral hazard, caused the real-estate bubble and triggered the 2007-08 financial global crisis.

In light of the evidence against lending practices, lenders, naturally, ought to learn from not applying the principles of the basic model discussed above; but, applying the principles entails, a reduction in the supply of credit and consequently in aggregate demand with negative, and perhaps long-lasting, implications for financial capital democratization and growth. To alleviate this problem, Hatzius (2008), points-out that it would be necessary to design government policies in order (i) to boost private lending and (ii) to guarantee sustained lending by the government-sponsored mortgage firms Fannie Mae and Freddie Mac.

As we move forward, Judge Richard Posner (June 2009) has recommended a systemic risk[1] measure and that responsibility to monitor systemic risk should be undertaken by the central bank. Federal Reserve Chairman Ben Bernanke has accepted the task under special conditions[2]. Unquestionably, a systemic measure to monitor and guard against systemic risk would guide future banks and contribute to the dampening of USA's bank-driven business cycle fluctuations in the future.

Endnotes

1. According to Posner (May 2009), "systemic risk is the risk imposed by inter-linkages and interdependencies in a system or market, which could potentially bankrupt or bring down the entire system or market if one player is eliminated, or a cluster of failures occurs at once. Systemic financial risk occurs when contingency plans that are developed individually to address selected risks are collectively incompatible."

2. According to Indiviglio (October 2009), "testifying before the House Financial Services Committee, Federal Reserve Chairman Ben Bernanke ...said that an oversight council should be in place to regulate the systemic risk of the U.S. financial system, rather than just the Federal Reserve. ... He believes the Fed should have sole responsibility for the consolidated supervision, but that a diverse panel of regulators should have oversight. The way to think of this is that the consolidated supervisor would handle all of the actual day-to-day work and rulemaking for systemically relevant firms. The oversight panel would attempt to identify new risk to the system, servicing a sort of big picture function."

References

Adams, W., L. Eivan, & J. Levin; "Liquidity Constraints and Imperfect Information in Subprime Lending", *American Economic Review*, March 2009, Vol. 99, #1, pp: 49-84.

Caballero, R.J., E. Farhi, P.O. Gourinchas; "Financial Crash, Commodity Prices and Global Imbalances", *Brookings Papers on Economic Activity*, Fall 2008, pp: 1-55.

Hatzius, J.; "Beyond Leverage Losses: The Balance Sheet Effects of the Home Price Downturn", *Brookings Papers on Economic Activity*, Fall 2008, pp: 195-228.

Jaffee, D., & T. Russell; "Imperfect Information, Uncertainty, and Credit Rationing", *Quarterly Journal of Economics*, Vol. 90, #4, pp: 651-666.

Indiviglio, D.; "An Elegant Statement of the Problem With Financial Markets", <http://business.theatlantic.com/2009/10/bernanke_sends_mixed_signals_for_systemic_risk_regulation.php#>, October 1, 2009.

Mayer, C., K. Pence, & Sherlund, S.M.; "The Rise in Mortgage Defaults", *Journal of Economic Perspectives*, Vol. 23, #1, Winter 2009, pp: 27-50.

O'Driscoll Jr., G. P.; "The Financial Crisis: Origins and Consequences", The Intercollegiate Review, Vol. 44, #2, Fall 2009, pp: 4-12.

Posner, R.A.; *Wall Street Journal*, May 2009.

Posner, R.A.; "A Failure of Capitalism", *The Atlantic Correspondents*, <http://correspondents.theatlantic.com/richard_posner/2009/06/financial_regulatory_reform_ii.php>, June 24, 2009.

Ramady, M.A and Demetri Kantarelis; "Financial capital democratisation: recipes for growth and disaster", *International Journal of Society Systems Science*, Vol. 1, # 4, 2009, pp. 325 – 350.

Chapter 4:

Torts

I. Introduction

According to competitive market principles, allocation efficiency is achieved when costs of products and services offered in markets are born by producing firms and are included, entirely, in selling prices; in other words, maximum efficiency gains are realized when producers internalize all costs. If producers externalize a portion of their costs, they would: be able to produce more (perhaps excessively); withhold incentives for R&D necessary for production process and physical capital innovation; sell at lower prices; encourage wasteful use of their products; discourage recycling; cause pollution, health problems, and wrongful accidents in the work place and in the outside stakeholder community. Needless to say that internalization of costs may be practiced not only by producers but, in a contributory fashion, by their stakeholders as well.

Of course, as it has been demonstrated by Ronald Coase (1960) when transaction costs are zero or negligible, the business firm may rely on clearly defined property rights and / or contracts (credible commitments) to deal with the violation of property and safety rights or, in other words, the internalizing of external costs between it and its various stakeholders. (See the Appendix at the end of this chapter for a graphical description of Coase's Invariance Theorem other than the descriptions offered in chapter 1.)

When transaction costs are high, the business firm would have to rely on tort liability laws. According to Cooter and Ulen (1996, p. 262), "the economic essence of tort law is its use of liability to internalize externalities created by high transaction costs." A tort is a 'wrong' committed by the firm against its stakeholders (or vice-versa) and it may range from inadvertent to deliberate, from severe to insignificant, from crime to irritation. For more on torts and liability laws see Brown (1973), Calabresi (1970), Posner (2007) and Shavell (1980, 1987). For definitions and examples see various web sites listed under Definitions/Examples.

In the remainder of this chapter, I assume that a business firm is the defendant responsible for precautionary safety in the workplace, and an employee, working for the firm, is the plaintiff. Would the firm (employee) have the incentive to provide (undertake) sufficient precaution? To answer this question, I rely on simple marginalist economics concepts and popular legal rules and compensation formulas. More specifically, I discuss incentive mechanisms for internalization of costs in conjunction with the well-known concepts of liability, negligence, precaution and methodologies for estimation of compensatory damages. The chapter's contribution is pedagogical in nature; with torts' examples and reliance on the Coase Theorem it aims to help law and economics students, as well as practitioners in law and regulation, to better understand the implications of various internalization schemes. In Section II, I deal with liability / negligence rules and in Section III with methodologies for estimation of compensatory damages; a summary / conclusion and an appendix follow thereafter.

II. Liability and Negligence

Precautionary measures may range from physical to various services and from medical to procedural. Precaution (undertaken by the firm or its employees) is an input in short supplies and, as such, it carries a cost; it also carries a benefit for all involved because the more of it becomes available the lower the expected harm. Naturally, the more precaution there is, the higher the costs that have to be paid by the provider, the lower the probability of harm and, as a result, the lower the expected harm. Hence, 'society' is burdened by two costs: outlays for precautionary measures (PC) and payments for damages or harms (H).

Let MPC = Marginal Precautionary Costs, MEH = Marginal Expected Harms and S = Level of Precaution. Where, MPC = f(S) with $f_S>0$; and MEH = g(S) with $g_S<0$. These "f" and "g" functions (which may be linear or non-linear) are graphed in Figure 1 below. In conjunction with Figure 1, consider the following tort rules:

II(1). Rule of No Liability

According to this tort rule, the firm is not liable for accidents in the work place; it has no obligation to offer any precaution over and above S_1, the "costless" minimum possible.

At S_1, the firm's total precautionary costs (TPC) equal zero and the total expected harms (TEH) to employees correspond to the area $S_1e_1S_2$. Hence, under this rule, the expected social cost of torts, E(T), is:

$$E(T)_{\text{No Liability}} = TPC + TEH = S_1e_1S_2. \qquad (1)$$

II(2). Rule of Strict Liability

According to this tort rule, the firm is strictly liable. Employees have no obligation to pay for any costs associated with accidents in the work place as long as the firm offers no less than S_2, the maximum possible level of precaution, characterized by zero marginal (and total) expected harms.

At S_2, the firm's TPC = $S_1e_2S_2$ and the employees' TEH equal zero. Hence, under this rule, the expected social cost of torts is:

$$E(T)_{\text{Strict Liability}} = TPC + TEH = S_1e_2S_2. \qquad (2)$$

Comparing (1) to (2) it is obvious that the firm would prefer the rule of "No Liability" and employees the rule of "Strict Liability". Under "No Liability", the firm has no incentive to introduce any precautionary measures; it passes on the cost – it imposes an externality - to its employees. Under "Strict Liability", the employee has no incentive to undertake any precaution in the work place, the firm, in this case, internalizes all costs.

Figure 1: Marginal Expected Harms and Marginal Precautionary Costs

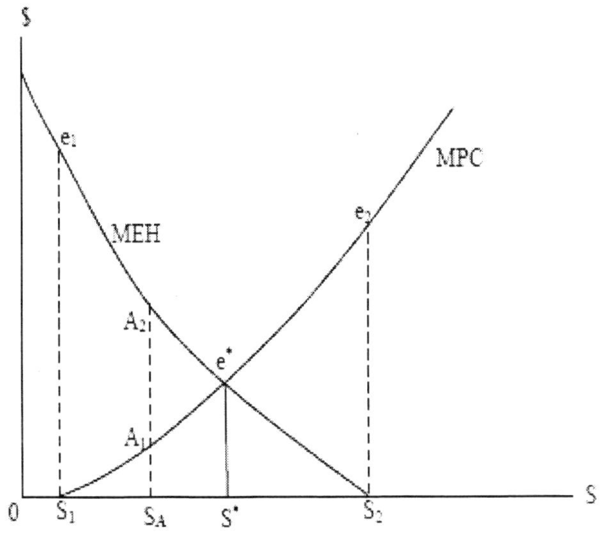

II(3). Rule of Bilateral Liability

Obviously, neither one of the above rules contributes to efficiency. A precaution level such as S^* (achieved through a rule of bilateral liability) would be less costly to society; notice that at S*,

$E(T)_{\text{Bilateral Liability}} = (S_1e^*S^* + S_2e^*S^*)$ and that,

$E(T)_{\text{Bilateral Liability}} < E(T)_{\text{No Liability}}$, as well as

$E(T)_{\text{Bilateral Liability}} =< E(T)_{\text{Strict Liability}}$.

Of course, bilateral liability is easier said than done: neither of the sides would have the incentive for efficient precaution; each, instead, would have the incentive to externalize to the other as much precautionary cost as possible. A possible way out of it is to establish legal standards and then, as explained below, rely on various negligence rules.

II(4). Rule of Negligence

Suppose the legal or regulation authorities have determined that the precaution standard is identical to the efficient precaution level of S^* in Figure 1. If the firm offers $S \geq S^*$, it is not liable for any compensation whatsoever; if it offers $S_A < S^*$ it is liable for the compensation that corresponds to the difference $(S^* - S_A)$.

If the firm chooses to operate at S_A, in other words not to comply with the law, it will save for itself $(S^*e^*A_1S_A)$ but it would have to pay a compensation of $(S^*e^*A_2S_A)$; because, in absolute value, the gain is less than the loss, the firm would have the incentive to comply at S^*. Naturally, unless the firm derives benefits associated with reputation, altruism and the like, it may not find it rational to expand precaution above S^*.

Of course, it is possible that injury in the work place is not due to negligence by the employer but due to lack of precaution by the employee. To minimize this problem, in addition to a precautionary standard imposed on the firm (S^*_F), authorities may impose a precautionary standard on employees (S^*_E) as well. Hence, in this case negligence may be modified as follows:

II(5). Rule of Contributory Negligence

If $S_F < S^*_F$ and $S_E \geq S^*_E$ ➔ Firm Liable;

If $S_F \geq S^*_F$ or $S_E < S^*_E$ ➔ Firm Not Liable.

II(6). Rule of Comparative Negligence

If $S_F < S^*_F$ and $S_E \geq S^*_E$ ➔ Firm Pays 100%;

If $S_F \geq S^*_F$ and $S_E < S^*_E$ ➔ Employee Pays 100%;

If $S_F < S^*_F$ and $S_E < S^*_E$ ➔ Firm and Employee Pay Proportionally.

Whatever each one of the entities pays is determined by the differences between standards and actual levels of precaution. Hence,

the negligent firm's proportion of liability is:

$(S^*_F - S_F) / [(S^*_F - S_F) + (S^*_E - S_E)]$; and,

the negligent employee's proportion of liability is:

$(S^*_E - S_E) / [(S^*_F - S_F) + (S^*_E - S_E)]$.

Hypotehticl Illustration:

Consider the following hypothetical illustration. Suppose a construction firm is building a multi-story structure; the firm is required to construct a canopy to protect the ground workers from falling debris and all workers are required to purchase and wear helmets. (Perhaps the firm does not make such helmets freely available to workers because of union regulations or because it wants its workers to have the incentive to undertake precaution in the work place over and above whatever precaution the firm itself may offer.) The canopy that satisfies the legal standard costs $50,000 but the firm, instead, installs a $30,000 canopy. Therefore, the extent of the firm's negligence is ($50,000 – $30,000) = $20,000.

A ground worker chooses not to wear a high quality $90 legal standard helmet but, instead, a $50 sub-standard one and, one day, she suffers a 'repairable' head injury by falling debris. Suppose, it has been determined, based on historical data, that the high quality $90 helmet reduces the likelihood of 'repairable' head injuries by (1/800) which implies that the implicit 'standard value of a head injury repair' (V) is V = 90 / (1/800) = $72,000. ($72,000 may be the amount needed, more or less, for medical expenses or compensation.) The worker could have purchased the high quality legal standard helmet, or even pay more for one of higher quality; instead, she opted to go (gamble) with a sub-standard helmet with a value of V = 50 / (1/800) = $40,000. Therefore, the extent of the worker's negligence is ($72,000 – $40,000) = $32,000. By making the choice to go with a lower value helmet, the worker is negligent against herself. Dividing all numbers by 1,000 and comparing, the negligent firm's proportion of liability is:

($50 – $30) / [($50 - $30) + ($72 – $40)] = 0.3846; and,

the negligent worker's proportion of liability is:

($72– $40) / [($50 - $30) + ($72 – $40)] = 0.6154.

Comparative Negligence has been criticized over the difficulty of computing proportions of liability. As the above hypothetical example illustrates, entities and legal authorities may have to rely on probability estimates from experimentation, collection of data without guarantee of certainty and deal with high administration costs. Additionally, if the disputing parties are not engaged in the same activity then it is more difficult to determine exact percentages of fault; litigants, in this case, would have to absorb high transaction costs due to prolonged negotiations, hostility, unreasonable behavior, politics and so on. At the end, the efficiency gains from a correct allocation of fault proportions may be outweighed by administration, transaction and other costs.

II(7). Rule of Strict Liability with Contributory Negligence

This rule assigns the cost of unintentional injury to the firm (the injurer), regardless of its level of precaution, unless the employee (the injured) is liable:

If $S_E < S^*_E$ → Firm Not Liable;

If $S_E \geq S^*_E$ → Firm Liable.

III. Methodologies for Estimation of Compensatory Damages

Although the liability and negligence analysis above centered on the firm and its employees, it was mentioned that similar disputes might arise between the firm and any of its stakeholders. The firm often is subjected to liability or negligence ranging from *product and/or service* to *loss of human life* for which an important aspect of litigation is the choice of methodology for estimation of compensatory damages.

For market products with substitutes, firms may rely on the ***indifference*** method to compute damages. For this method to work, the 'victimized' client must be indifferent between the product/service offered by the 'injuring' firm and a similar product/service offered by another firm. Hence, the liable or negligible firm may perfectly compensate the client so that she uses the money to buy a substitute product/service from another firm in the market.

III(1). Optimal Commitments to Performance and Reliance [1]

A deal between entities X and Y may induce both to invest. If X is the promisor and Y the promisee, X may invest in performing and Y in reliance upon the promise. To illustrate, consider a deal for renovation between X (a building construction company) and Y (the owner of a hospital building in need of renovation and extension.) To fulfill the promise, X may have to invest, *in advance*, in specific construction equipment, which it does not currently possess. In anticipation of the final project, Y may invest, *in advance as well*, in additional medicine service inputs ranging from human (hiring doctors, nurses and administrators) to physical (purchasing computers and special machinery for medical procedures.) Obviously, X and Y would be fully interdependent upon each other and the possibility of breaching would motivate them to consider possible compensation remedies with different incentive implications for investments in performance and reliance. In the end, the promisor and the promisee should include optimal commitments to performance and reliance. Optimality, of course, requires accurate estimation of damages and it may involve third parties such as private arbitrators, courts or even government representatives.

Damages, paid by the promisor, may be computed on the basis of:

(1) Perfect Expectations.

(These damages leave the promisee *indifferent between performance and breach*);

(2) Perfect Reliance.

(These damages leave the promisee *indifferent between no deal and breach*);

(3) Perfect Opportunity-Cost.

These damages leave the promisee *indifferent between breach and performance of the best alternative deal.*

Similarly, for damages paid by the promisee.

For example, consider the builder / hospital entities used for illustration above in conjunction with Figure 2. The builder may deliver a building ranging from dysfunctional (0) to perfectly functional (100%) and damages may be computed subject to three possible indifference curves: perfect expectations (E), perfect reliance (R), or perfect-opportunity cost (OC). Each indifference curve connects a set of combinations that have the same utility; each combination corresponds to a certain dollar figure on the vertical axis and the corresponding percentage functionality of the building on the horizontal axis.

First, assume that the deal between X and Y requires perfect expectations damages, in other words the possibilities associated with curve E. If the builder delivers a 100% perfectly functional building, the hospital owner would be happy and there would be no basis for remuneration. But if, in the end, the building were only 25% functional, the hospital owner would be equally happy only if, in addition, it receives a $20 million compensation for damages from the builder.

Second, assume that, prior to renovation, the building's functionality is 50% and that the deal between X and Y requires perfect reliance damages, or the possibilities associated with curve R. If the builder delivers a 50% functional building (as it used to be prior to the deal), the hospital owner would be happy and there would be no basis for remuneration. But if, in the end, the building were only 25% functional, the hospital owner would be equally happy only if, in addition, it receives a $9 million compensation for damages from the builder.

Third, assume that the hospital owner, instead, could have hired a competing builder who would have renovated the building for 80% functionality. In this case, the deal between Y and X requires that if X does not deliver at least 80% functionality, Y is entitled to remuneration. Thus, the deal between X and Y requires perfect opportunity-cost damages, or the possibilities associated with curve OC. If the builder delivers an 80% functional building (as the competing builder would do prior to the deal), the hospital owner would be happy and there would be no basis for remuneration. But if, in the end, the building is only 25% functional, the hospital owner would be equally happy only if, in addition, it receives a $17 million compensation for damages from the builder.

In addition to the above compensation schemes, the dealing parties may consider, among other: (a) *restitution* (it requires that the promisee receives back what it gave to a breaching promisor for

Figure 2: Damages Based on Expectations, Reliance and Opportunity.

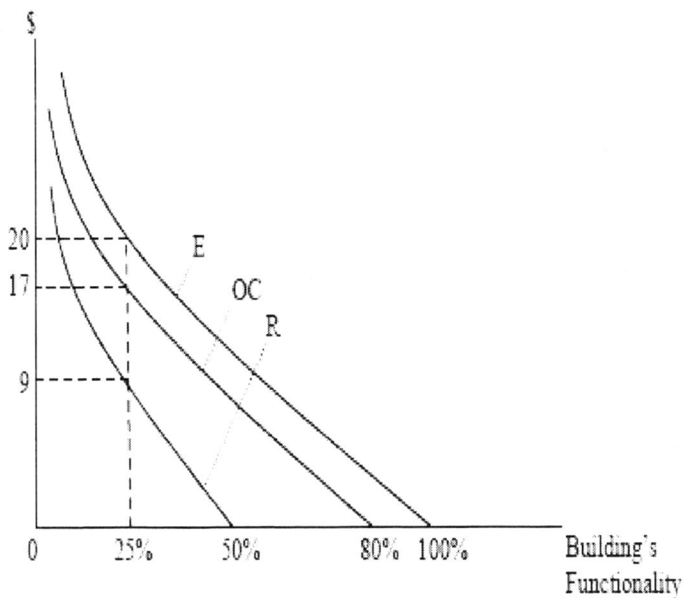

the deal – for example, a down payment;) and (b) *disgorgement* (compensation received by the promisee equal to the profit made by the promisor for misconduct – for example, promisor X promises to deliver a service to promisee Y but instead it delivers the service to someone else.)

III(2). Risk-equivalence

Of course there are 'goods' for which there are no markets for substitutes. For example, for injuries involving loss of life or a limb, compensation would be difficult to estimate and most of the time the estimated amounts are far from perfect either in favor or against the plaintiff (defendant.) Despite the difficulties though, legal institutions have to award damages for wrongful death or for grievous personal injuries. A method often used (conceptually easy but practically complex and controversial) is the method of ***risk-equivalence***, which was just used, in the hypothetical illustration, to demonstrate comparative negligence. It takes actual market sales as a guide to how much the client values safety. For example, suppose that a car buyer purchases a car with anti-lock brakes and pays the asking price plus \$X to the seller. If the \$X extra expense on anti-lock brakes reduces the likelihood of deadly accident by (P_A) then the consumer's valuation of safety, which implies an implicit value of life (V_{Life}) is:

$$V_{Life} = (\$X) / (P_A).$$

For illustration, if \$X = \$2,000 and $P_A = (1/7{,}000)$, then

$$V_{Life} = (\$2{,}000) / (1/7{,}000) = \$14{,}000{,}000.$$

Hence, if after a deadly car accident, in which only the car/driver owner was killed, it is determined that the death was due to the failed anti-lock brakes (and not due to other causes such as excessive speeding, or driving under the influence of alcohol, etc.) that the driver had paid for, the car manufacturer would be found at fault and would have to pay $14,000,000 in damages for wrongful death to the beneficiaries of the victim.

Undoubtedly, easier said than done: Do probabilities like P_A exist? How accurate are they? Does value of life involve other things: lost estimated future income of the victim (another estimate!) and the discount rate to be used, hedonic variables such lost pleasures for the remaining of life, and so on. [2]

IV. Summary & Conclusion

Assuming that a firm is the defendant responsible for precautionary safety in the workplace, and an employee, working for the firm, is the plaintiff, I explored under what conditions the firm (employee) would have the incentive to provide (undertake) sufficient precaution for the purpose of cost internalization. By relying on simple marginalist economic concepts, popular legal rules and compensation formulas the main conclusions may be summarized as follows:

- Internalization of costs may be practiced not only by producers but, in a contributory fashion, by their stakeholders as well.
- When transaction costs are zero or negligible (see Coase), the business firm may rely on clearly defined property rights and / or contracts (credible commitments) to deal with the violation of property and safety rights or, in other words, the internalizing of external costs between it and its various stake holders.
- When transaction costs are high, the business firm would have to rely on tort liability laws.
- Neither "No Liability" or "Strict Liability" contributes to efficiency.
- A precaution level achieved through a rule of "Bilateral Liability" would be less costly to society but neither one of

the sides would have the incentive for efficient precaution. A possible way out of it is to establish legal standards of precaution for both parties and then rely on various negligence rules such as contributory and comparative.

- Damages may be computed on the basis of Perfect Expectations, Perfect Reliance and Perfect Opportunity-Cost.
- For injuries involving loss of life or a limb, compensation would be difficult to estimate. A method often used is the method of *risk-equivalence*, which takes actual market sales as a guide to how much the client values safety.

It is hoped that the pedagogical exercise in this chapter would prove helpful to law and economics students as well as practitioners in law and regulation as they endeavor to understand the implications of various internalization schemes for more efficient outcomes. Naturally, a follow up to the exercise undertaken in this chapter could be a study of real-world legal cases, preferably from around the world, with the objective to empirically validate or refute the strengths and weaknesses of the proposed incentive mechanisms.

Endnotes

1. Sections III(1), III(2) and the Appendix draw heavily from Cooter and Ulen (1996); to fit the purpose of this paper, the analysis differs with respect to examples and other modifications.

2. Alternatively, compensation may be based on traditional measurements of benefits and costs subject to inflation rates (p) and controversial - due to subjectivity - discount factors (r) (where r stands for opportunity cost.) For example, the option of a lawsuit may be feasible only when $(PV_B / PV_C) > 1$ or when $(PV_B - PV_C) > 0$, where PV = present value, B=benefit (from compensation), and C=cost (from, primarily, legal fees.) Such benefits and costs may be measured as explained below.

Measurement of Benefits & Costs

B_t = benefit, $t = 0, 1, \ldots T$

C_t = cost, $t = 0, 1, \ldots T$

p = inflation rate

r_s = social discount rate

b = real dollars benefit

$b_t = B_t / (1+p)^t$

$$\mathbf{PV_B = PV\ of\ Benefits = \Sigma\ [b_t / (1+r_s)^t]}$$

c = real dollars cost

$c_t = C_t / (1+p)^t$

$$\mathbf{PV_C = PV\ of\ Costs = \Sigma\ [c_t / (1+r_s)^t]}$$

<u>Determining Feasibility</u>

(PV_B / PV_C) = **Benefit – Cost Ratio**

If $(PV_B / PV_C) > 1$, the option is considered feasible.

$(PV_B - PV_C)$ = **PV of Net Benefits**

If $(PV_B - PV_C) > 0$, the option is considered feasible.

Appendix: Coase's Invariance Theorem

Ronald Coase (1960) suggested that a solution to the problem of negative externalities due to environmental pollution is not necessary. Assuming that economic agents are free to negotiate – pollutees can pay the polluter to reduce pollution or the polluter can bribe the pollutees to accept more pollution – Coase showed that the same amount of output and pollution would be produced, regardless of which side owned the rights to clean air or water or, in general, property affected. If the polluter owned the right to clean property, the pollutee would pay until the marginal benefit from emission reduction equaled the marginal cost. If the pollutee owned the right to clean property, the polluter would pay until the marginal cost equaled the marginal benefit of less emission. Hence, with zero or insignificant obstacles to bargaining (zero or insignificant bargaining-related transaction costs), the parties involved would reach the same Pareto optimal levels of output and emission. The only dissimilarity would be an equity issue: who pays whom for the right to make use of the property.

Assuming zero transaction costs, well defined property rights and a perfectly competitive market, Coase's invariance prediction may be illustrated with two entities one of which, the polluter, is a firm and the other, the pollutee, is the entire community. In this case, the firm may impose on the community a negative externality equal to the difference between social marginal cost (SMC) and private marginal cost (MC). The cost associated with this negative externality, may be absorbed by the firm (the firm may internalize the externality) or paid by the community (the community may compensate the firm for investing in 'green' production technology.) Obviously, if the firm and the community experience no obstacles in possible negotiations with each other (zero transaction costs) they will reach a more or less equitable compromised agreement regardless of how property rights are initially distributed among themselves. If transaction costs are high, the legal system may be used for the generation of reasonable and enforceable property laws, which in turn will affect the distribution of the externality costs.

Consider Figure 3. The firm produces Q and faces demand (D) which is fixed at the ongoing market product price of P. (AR=average revenue and MR=marginal revenue.)

Suppose the firm may produce Q with or without emissions. If it produces without emissions, it sets MR = MC to maximize profit at Q^* for a maximum profit of aP0. When the firm produces with emissions, the emission cost may be paid in full or in part by the firm itself (in which case the firm internalizes the cost) or by the surrounding community (in which case the firm externalizes the cost.) Consider the following settings involving a polluting firm whose emissions are not deadly.

Figure 3: External Costs

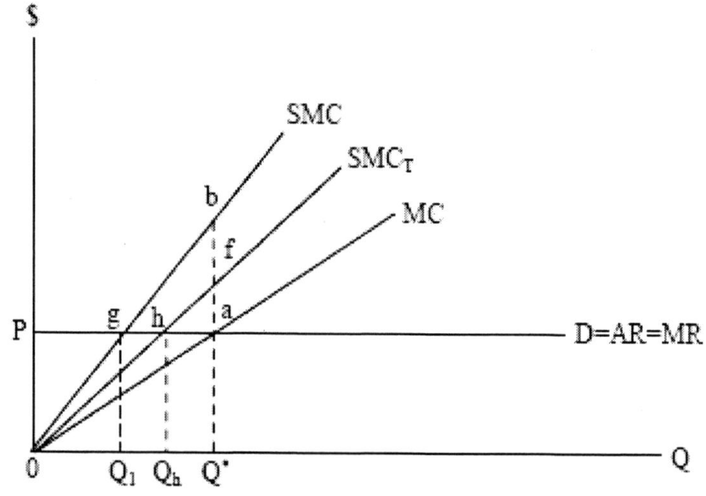

Setting I: the law does not restrict the firm from polluting. In this setting, the polluting firm will maximize profit subject to its private marginal cost (MC), sell Q^* and realize a profit of aP0; because it is free to pollute, the pollution it causes (the negative externality) will be paid by the community. The community will pay P for Q^* plus the difference between SMC and MC or, P+ba. For all units up to Q^*, the total externality cost is the triangle 0ba. The community, in this case, may alleviate the burden of the externality cost by subsidizing the firm to install "green" production technology, which may reduce SMC to SMC_T. At SMC_T, for all units up to Q^*, the total externality cost is the triangle 0fa which is less than the previous triangle 0ba. Thus, in this setting it pays for the community to subsidize (or bribe) the polluter to pollute less. The firm ends up with the same profit, the community ends up paying less externality costs and, overall, well-being improves.

Setting II: by law, the community has the right to clean environment. In this setting, the polluting firm has to internalize the emission cost; in other words, its true marginal cost will be the one designated SMC. Thus, subject to SMC, the firm makes a profit of gP0 and the community, although it still pays P it buys Q_1, which is less than Q^*, but it experiences no externality costs whatsoever. In this case, the polluting firm has the incentive to invest in "green" producing technology; such investing will rotate the SMC to SMC_T (as in Setting I above.) With SMC_T, the firm's profit will increase to hP0 while consumers will purchase more output at the same price.

References

Brown, J. (1973). "Toward An Economic Theory of Liability," Journal of Legal Studies 2:323-349.

Calabresi, Guido, (1970), *The Cost of Accidents: A Legal and Economic Analysis*, Yale University Press, USA.

Coase, Ronald, (1960). "The Problem of Social Cost," *Journal of Law and Economics* 3:1-44.

Cooter, R. and Ulen, T. (1996), *Law and Economics*, 2nd ed., Addison-Wesley, USA.

Definitions / Examples
<http://www.psychservices.psychiatryonline.org/cgi/content/full/51/6/817-a>
<http://www.the-injury-lawyer-directory.com/negligence.html>
<http://www.contributorynegligence.org/>

Posner, Richard A., (2007), *Economic Analysis of Law, 7th ed.*, Aspen Publishers, USA.

Shavell, Steven, (1980), "Strict Liability versus Negligence", Journal of Legal Studies, Vol. 9, 1-25.

Shavell, Steven, (1987), *Economic Analysis of Accident Law*, Harvard University Press, USA.

Chapter 5:

Occupational Stress - Potential for Tort Litigation

I. Introduction

I.1. Reality in the USA

According to the National Institute for Occupational Safety and Health (NIOSH) (2002), "job stress can be defined as the harmful physical and emotional responses that occur when the requirements of the job do not match the capabilities, resources, or needs of the worker." Sweeney et al (1991) identify six factors that contribute to work-related stress: professional value, support, demands, tasks, resources, and rewards. Many of the factors were management issues and related to staffing levels, time management, availability of resources, supervision levels, rewards, and recognition.[1]

As stressed by NIOSH (a) health care expenditures are nearly 50% greater for workers who report high levels of stress; and (b) studies show that stressful working conditions have a negative effect on the bottom line. A study conducted by Blumenthal et al (2002), reports that cardiac patients who are taught to manage their stress enjoy better health at less health care cost than patients who participate in an exercise program or those given typical heart treatment. In other words, society clearly gains from lower health care costs and, as one may easily infer from the results, from improved productivity in the work place as well.

In another report by Higbie (2001), according to the federal Bureau of Labor Statistics, "Stress costs American business about $10,000 annually per employee, in absenteeism, lower productivity and increasing health and workers' compensation costs, with an overall economic impact of about $300 billion, … (and it) is the No. 1 reason for worker disability." According to Higbie, firms have been offering in house, stress management classes, office massages, nap times to mention a few, all of which take away production time. Additionally, some firms share with their employees stress reduction costs, after the workday is over, such as membership fees for laughter, dancing and exercise clubs. In general, according to Higbie and a web reference in her piece (Stressdirections.com), firms have discovered that stress reduction efforts, although costly, contribute to productivity increases enabling firms to experience reductions in losses and, perhaps, increases in profits.

Although for business firms, psychologists and NIOSH, the connections between occupational stress, productivity and wellbeing are not new, economists, as far as I know, have ignored the study of these links. The Blumenthal et al study mentioned above was conducted by a group of psychologists and other professionals. Another psychological study, by Revicki et al (1997), has studied work-related stress encountered by medical doctors who, compared with other working people, experience some of the highest stress levels. According to Revicki at al (p.30) "(w)orking with intensely emotional aspects of medical care, such as suffering, fear, and death, severe physical trauma, and in conditions where the outcomes of medical treatment are uncertain, contributes to a stressful environment… Physicians in training may be even more vulnerable … (and) … (e)mergency medicine physicians … may experience more stressful situations than do primary care physicians." Revicki at al (p. 33) summarize their findings as follows: "Work group support, role ambiguity, and work-related stress exert a direct influence on job satisfaction. Internal locus of control, peer support, and work-group support directly affect role ambiguity, which in turn influence work-related stress, depression, and satisfaction with work. Occupational stress and, to a lesser extent, role ambiguity, directly affect the development of depressive symptoms." Along the same lines, NIOSH highlights in its web page that according to the Journal of Applied Psychology, the "St. Paul and Marine Insurance

Company conducted several studies on the effects of stress prevention programs in hospital settings. Program activities included (1) employee and management education on job stress, (2) changes in hospital policies and procedures to reduce organizational sources of stress, and (3) establishment of employee assistance programs. In one study, the frequency of medication errors declined by 50% after prevention activities was implemented in a 700-bed hospital. In a second study, there was a 70% reduction in malpractice claims in 22 hospitals that implemented stress prevention activities. In contrast, there was no reduction in claims in a matched group of 22 hospitals that did not implement stress prevention activities."

1.2. Reality in the UK

In the UK things have gone a step further. As a recent front newspaper headline reads "Firms that ignore stress risks face legal action." According to Laurance (2003), the author of the article headed by the above headline, the Health and Safety Executive (HSE) of the British government has recommended a tough stress code-type regulation according to which firms would have to meet guidelines to avoid subjecting their employees to work stress. More specifically, the code "sets six standards aimed at easing the pressure and improving the quality of life in the office and on the shopfloor" ranging from job demands and control to input in organizational changes.

The six standards are centered around the following questions and their corresponding percentages Xi% (i=1,…,6.) If Xi% or more employees in a firm agree that each standard has been met, the firm will pass the assessment test:

- *Can employees cope with the demands of the job? (85%;)*
- *Do employees have control, an adequate say, over how they do their work? (85%;)*
- *Do employees get adequate support from colleagues and supervisors? (85%;)*
- *Do employees enjoy harmonious relationships with other employees or are subject to unacceptable behavior such as bullying? (65%;)*
- *Do employees understand their roles and responsibilities? (65%;)*
- *Are employees involved in organizational restructuring and change? (65%).*

As Laurence explains in the same article, "…Companies are being invited to implement the standards, piloted in 4 firms, from today (June 16, 2003.) The standards will be fine-tuned until the code is formally launched next year. The code is based on evidence from the seminal *Whitehall II* study of 10,000 civil servants who have been followed since 1985. The study, by Professor Sir Michael Marmot and colleagues of University College London, found staff could cope with high-pressure work environments, without damage to their health, provided they had a high degree of control over their working lives and good social support."[2]

My purpose in this chapter is to propose some neo-classical microeconomic theoretical concepts (sections II to IV) that describe issues associated with stress management in the work place. In section V, I recommend a Bayesian testing procedure followed by a summary and conclusion in section VI.

II. Optimum Stress without Regulation

A firm may be guided by the following model in search for S*, the optimum level of stress in the work place. Perhaps a firm, any firm (especially health care providers, private security agencies, air traffic controllers, and other such high stress entities) might choose to view stress (S) as a factor of production needed to produce a service or good Q; this implies that Q may be expressed as a function of S or,

$$Q = Q(S). \qquad (1)$$

A graph for (1), depicting a quadratic relationship, may be seen in Figure 1; in this Figure, Q is maximized at S_1. Depending on the occupation at hand, the left intercept of function (1) may be at the origin (e.g. as it may be for the profession of security officers) or at a point above zero on the vertical axis (e.g. as it may be for office secretaries.)

To examine whether or not S_1 is optimum, the firm may consider a map of 'n' isoprofit sets (or curves) such as

$$A_i = A_i(S, Q) \qquad (2)$$

where A_i = fixed level of profit; i=1,2,…n;

$\partial \Pi_i / \partial S < 0 and \partial \Pi_i / \partial Q > 0$; and $A_1 < A_2 < A_3 < \ldots$

These isoprofit curves are positively sloped and they are related negatively to S and positively to Q. The firm then may choose to maximize profit, function (2), subject to function (1), the stress production function or: Maximize $A_i = A_i(S, Q)$ subject to $Q = Q(S)$.

Assuming that the isoprofit curves are parallel to each other, that they do not cross each other and that they are shaped as those in Figure 2, the firm becomes better off when it moves northwest, in the direction of the arrow; thus, the locus $A_1(S, Q)$ corresponds to a lower profit than the locus $A_2(S, Q)$ and so forth.

Figure 2 summarizes the optimization results: (a) the profit maximizing stress level is less than the stress level that maximizes output: $S^* < S_1$; (b) at S^*, the firm produces less output than at S_1 but it realizes more profit: $A_2 > A_1$. Given the news in the popular press and the professional psychological studies cited above, it appears that this simple model finds some empirical support in the USA and the UK.

Figure 1: The 'Stress' production function

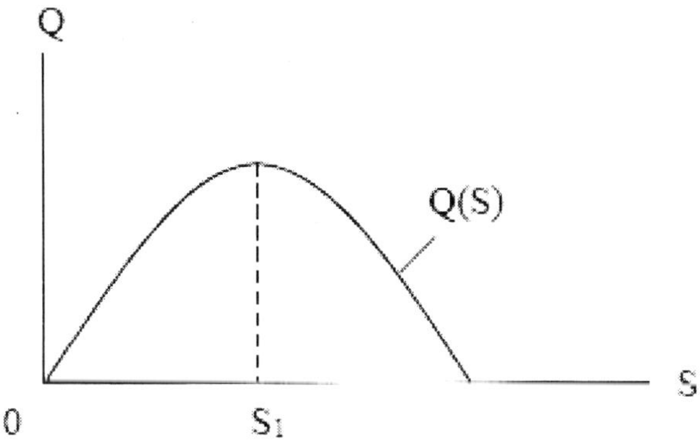

Figure 2: Optimum 'Stress'

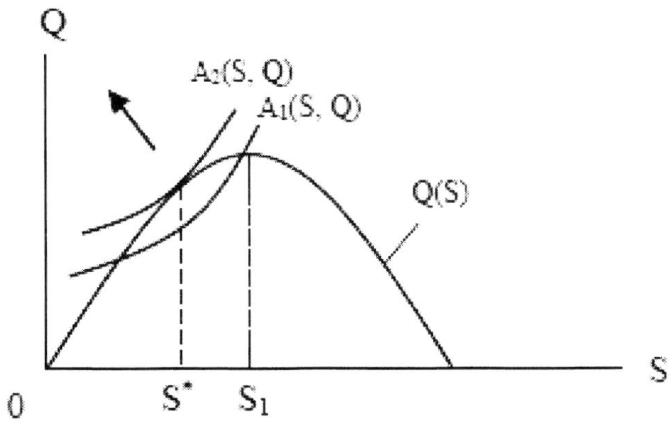

III. Sharing Costs

Without a doubt, air-traffic controllers and security officers get paid more than retail clerks not only because of the special skills they possess but also because of the high stress they experience in their efforts to seamlessly produce their vital services. In turn, employees that receive high wages for extra stress may spend a portion of their higher wages for the relief of stress. If employers do not pay their employees higher wages for the relief of stress, employees may impose costs on firms via absenteeism, high turnover and, in general, lower productivity.

Consider a stress reduction service such as a membership to a gym or a tennis/golf club or other clubs. The cost for stress reduction may be paid entirely by the employer or the employee; alternatively, they may share it. When a firm pays for the relief of stress it inflicts on its employees, its marginal stress relief cost (MRC) may be expressed as a negative function of stress (S); such a relationship is shown in Figure 3. At point S_f, the firm's total stress relief cost (TRC) is zero. At point S_r, the firm's TRC is equal to the area S_rKS_f. Rationally, an unregulated firm would be willing to pay something for the relief of stress in the work place if its profit improves. (More on this below.)

When an employee pays for the damages caused by stress in the work place, her marginal stress damages (MD) may be expressed as a positive function of stress (S); such a relationship is shown in Figure 4. Point S_t corresponds to the point of stress that the employee may tolerate without any damages; hence, at S_t, the employee's total stress damages (TD) is zero. At point S_d, the employee's TD is equal to the area S_tZS_d. Rationally, an employee would prefer less work stress to more.

Figure 3

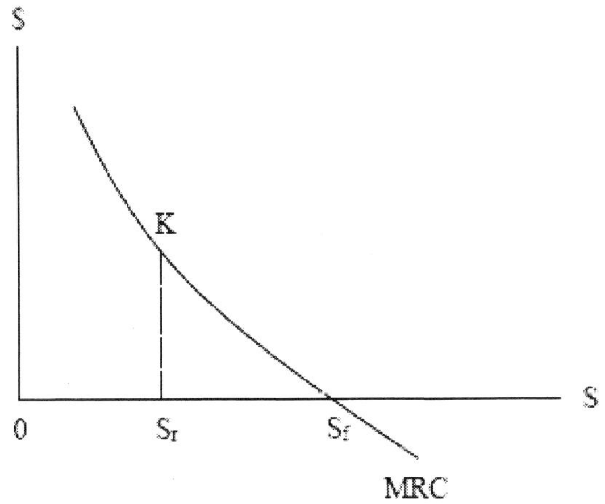

Figure 4

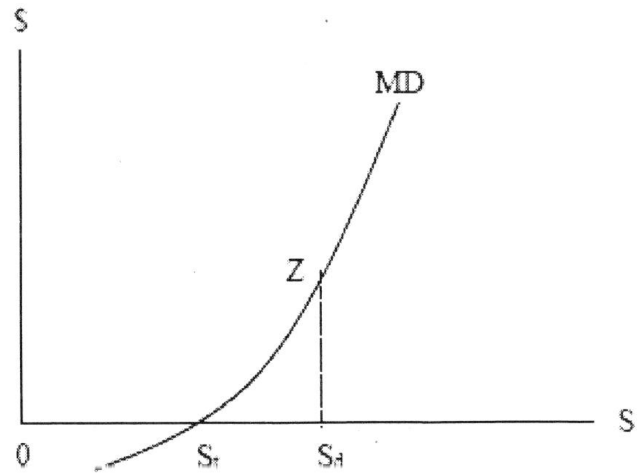

If the employer and the employee were to share stress costs, then setting MRC equal to MD would enable them to compute S_e (see Figure 5), the point at which the sum of TRC and TD is minimized. At S_e, the cost paid by the employer would be the area $S_f e S_e$ and the cost paid by the employee would be the area $S_t e S_e$. If the employee alone were to pay for all stress damages imposed upon her, she would pay $S_t L S_f$. Similarly, if the firm alone were to pay for all the stress relief cost so that stress is reduced down to S_t (the tolerable level), it would have to pay $S_f M S_t$. Hence, sharing stress relief costs is a cost efficient solution: the sum of shared costs ($S_t e S_f$) is less than the cost paid by the employee alone ($S_t L S_f$) or the firm alone ($S_f M S_t$.)

Figure 5

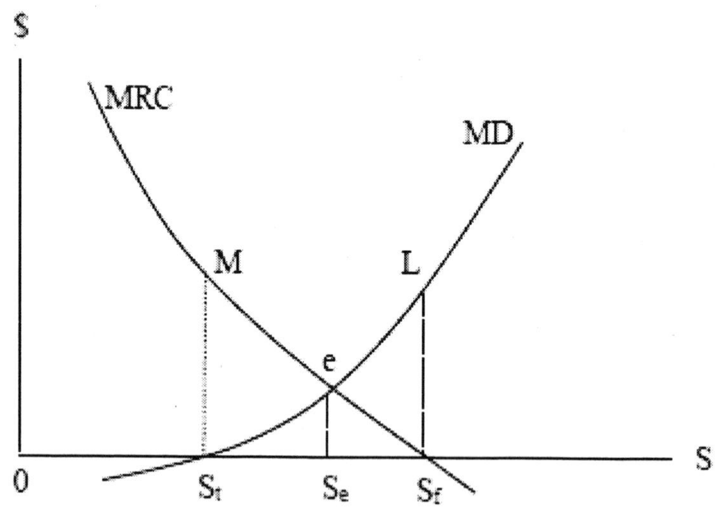

IV. Guided by a Standard

The analysis in the previous section points out that the level of stress that corresponds to Se may be justified as a *standard* for, firstly, the reallocation of stress within the firm, secondly, for guiding the firm to higher productivity and profit and, thirdly, for governmental regulation.

IV.1. Reallocation of Stress within the Firm

Suppose employees pay themselves for the relief of stress they experience in the work place and that the employer has determined and informed them that the profit maximizing stress level is S*. Consider Figure 6. Let the Figure portray two groups of employees, A in the upper panel (e.g. employees who are parents) and B in the lower panel (e.g. employees who are not parents.) Currently, A experiences stress S_{1A}, with damage costs $S_{0A}Z_AS_{1A}$ and, B S_{1B}, with damage costs $S_{0B}Z_BS_{1B}$. The sum of S_{1A} and S_{1B} equals S* but, the same S* level may be achieved if B takes on more stressful tasks (to relief A) and A, in turn, is offered less stressful tasks. For example, A may move from S_{1A} to S* and experience a reduction in stress costs (gain) equal to $S_{1A}Z_AQ_AS^*$; B may move from S_{1B} to S* and experience an increase in stress costs (loss) equal to $S_{1B}Z_BQ_BS^*$. Thus, given the slopes of the respective MD curves in Figure 6, the reallocation of stressful tasks reduces the overall total damages due to stress since the absolute value of the gain exceeds the absolute value of the loss.

This result, of course, depends on whether or not (i) such groupings of employees can take place, (ii) precise information about marginal damages exists, (iii) managerial ability, (iv) employee relations and the like. Given the nature of groups A and B above, most likely parent employees will appreciate a more flexible work schedule and parental leave relative to non-parent employees who may be willing to pick up the slack.

Similarly, S*, the profit maximizing S, may require the firm to pay for more stress relief in one production plant and for less in another. Consider Figure 7. Let the Figure portray two production plants that belong to the same firm, C in the upper panel (e.g. the 'less stressful' plant) and D in the lower panel (e.g. the 'more stressful' plant) Currently, C experiences stress S_{1C}, with relief costs $S_{0C}Z_CS_{1C}$ and, D S_{1D}, with relief costs $S_{0D}Z_DS_{1D}$. The sum of S_{1C} and S_{1D} equals S* but, the same S* level may be achieved if C is forced to experience more stress (to relief D) and D, in turn, is forced to experience less stress. For example, C may move from S_{1C} to S* and experience a decrease in stress relief costs (gain) equal to $S_{1C}Z_CQ_CS^*$; D may move from S_{1D} to S* and experience an increase in stress costs (loss) equal to $S_{1D}Z_DQ_DS^*$. Thus, given the slopes of the respective MRC curves in Figure 7, the reallocation of stress relief costs among production plans reduces the total stress relief costs since, as above, the absolute value of the gain exceeds the absolute value of the loss.

Figure 6

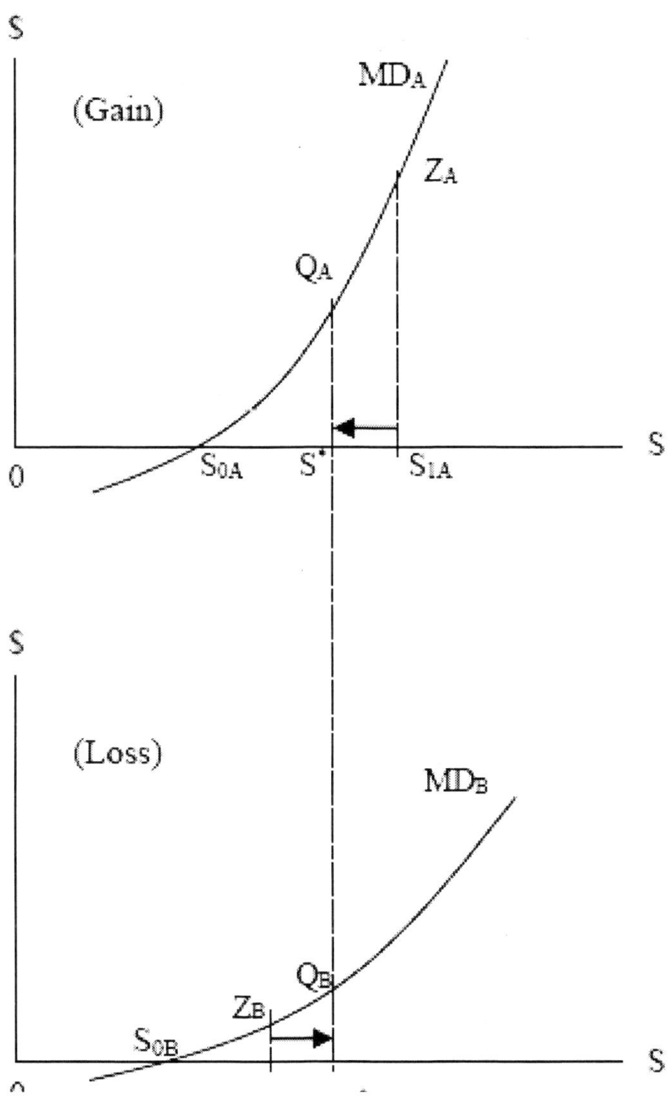

Figure 7

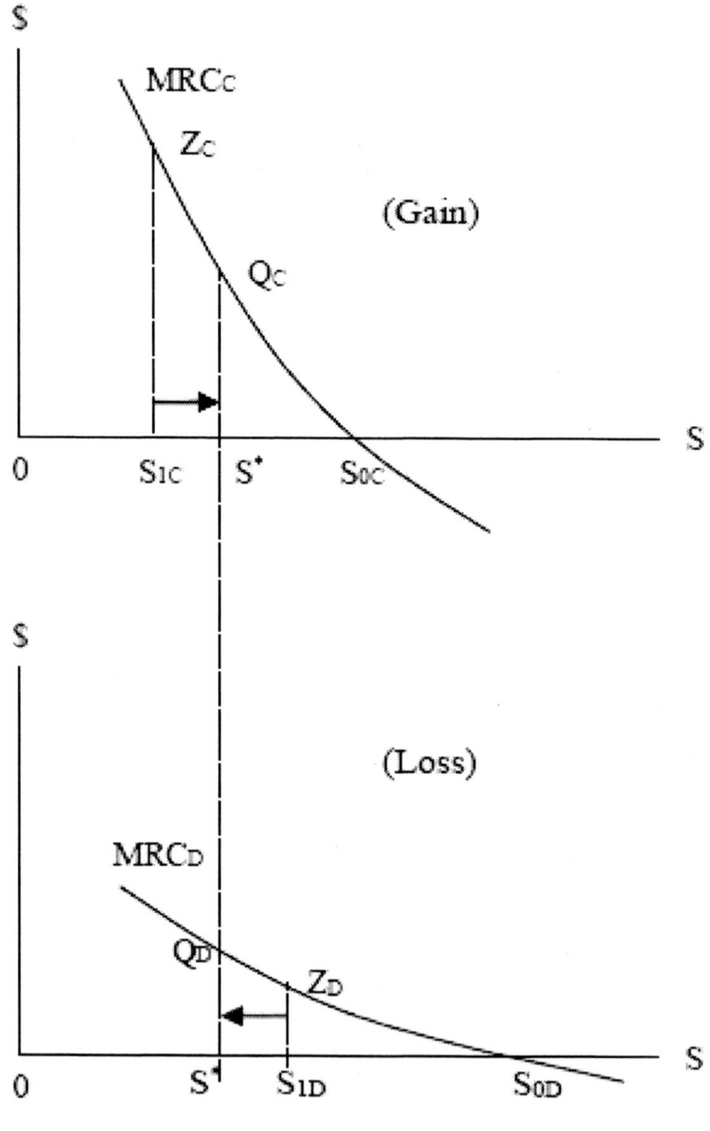

IV.2 Stress Relief for Higher Productivity and Profit

Would the firm have the incentive to pay for stress relief in an environment free of governmental regulation? The logical answer to this question is *yes* if stress reduction improves productivity and profit. Consider Figure 8, which combines Figures 2 and 5. According to the model described in section II above, a non-regulated firm would maximize profit at S_0 forcing its employees to absorb all costs associated with stress damages at S_0 (area S_tLS_0.) Alternatively, if a firm credibly estimates that a reduction in stress would cause an upward rotation of the Q(S) to Q'(S) around the origin, in other words improve productivity, the firm may decide to pay S_0eS_1 in relief so that S decrease from S_0 to S_1. At S_1, the firm reaches a higher profit level and a higher output level; simultaneously, the employee experiences a reduction in stress damages equal to the area S_0eL.

Naturally, one may ask: why stop at S_1? The answer is that S_1 is the most efficient point. Any other S level would generate higher total stress costs (costs paid by both employers and employees.) Without a doubt, stress cost sharing would be an efficient solution. In an environment without governmental regulation, the employer and the employee should always search for a point like S_1.

Figure 8

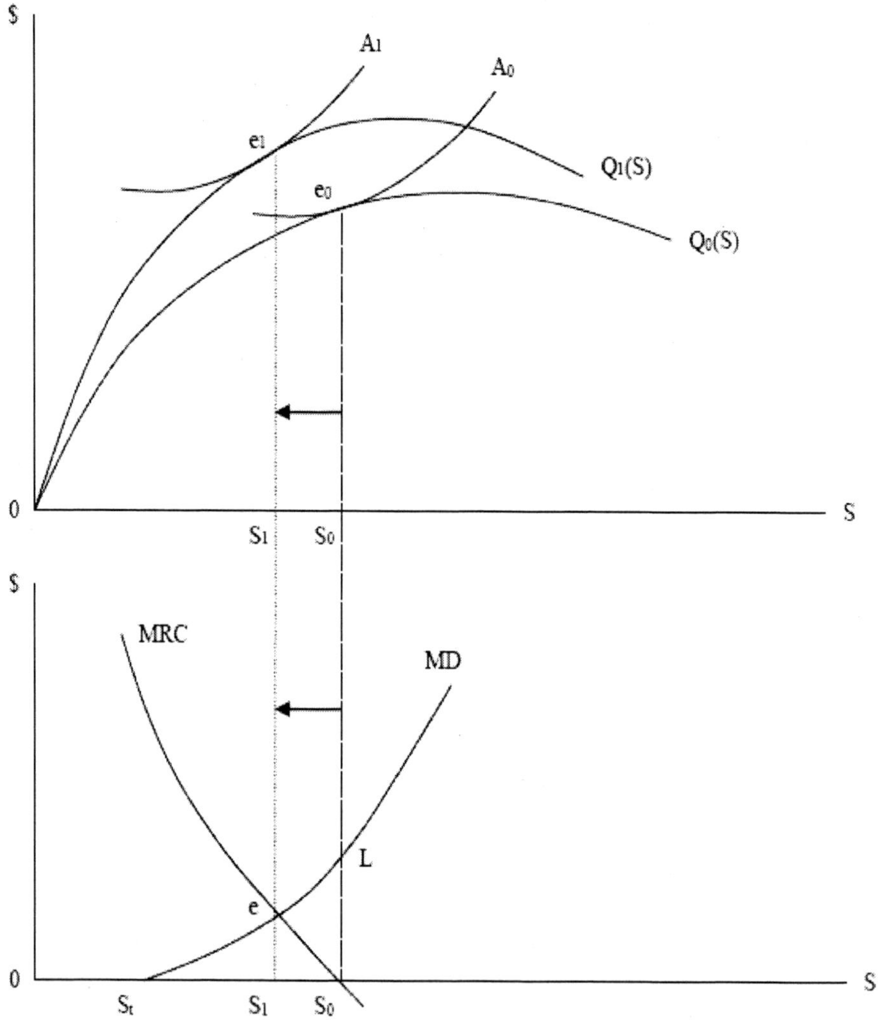

IV.3. Governmental Regulation

Although the above analysis implies that 'sharing' stress costs would be the correct way to go, it is likely that government, as pointed out above in the section dealing with reality in the UK, may decide to intervene by imposing standards. Consider Figure 9, which portrays a firm's profit as a function of stress (S.) Let A_f=profit without regulation and A_r=profit with regulation. As implied above, following the A_f curve, the unregulated firm will choose S* to maximize profit. Under regulation, the government may impose a standard according to which S should be no more than S_{r1}. If S is more than S_{r1}, the firm will pay a penalty that shifts a portion of its profit curve down from $A_3A_4A_5$ to $B_1B_2B_3$. If the firm inflicts a stress level of S_{r1} or less, its profit function will be given by $A_1A_2A_3$ as before. Hence, compliance with the standard guarantees to the firm the profit level that corresponds to A_3. In general, given a penalty for non-compliance, only standards that allow for profit above the profit level that corresponds to B_2 would be effective in forcing the firm to decrease stress in the work place. For example, the firm would not have the incentive to comply if the regulatory authority makes the mistake to set the standard at S_{r2}, in which case, the firm would rather raise the stress level up to S^*, pay the penalty and still end up with more profit at B_2 than at A_2.

Figure 9

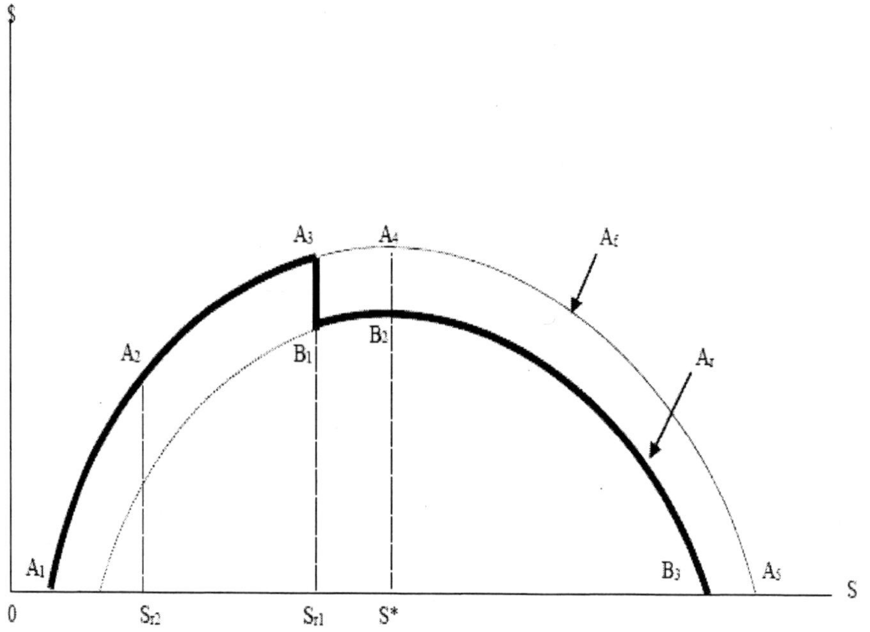

V. Bayesian Testing

Because it would be difficult for a firm to come up with precise estimates of the key functions (1) and (2) described in section II above, an alternative way to measure stress would be to use periodic screening of employees in conjunction with production procedures constantly adapted to changes. For such a periodic screening, a firm may rely on the Bayesian probabilistic methodology developed by Thomas Bayes, the legendary English clergyman / mathematician of the late 1700s. (For more details see Kantarelis et al, 2004.) Bayes' theorem is valuable because it enables us to recalculate a probability based on some new information. Bayesian analysis necessitates two steps: the first step requires that the decision-maker computes prior probabilities based on *population* information; the second step enables the decision-maker to compute a posterior probability as a function of the prior probability and the results of an experiment (e.g. the results of a screening test.)

Consider an imaginary illustration. A private hospital would like to consider changing the working conditions for its 1000 nurses so that they experience less occupational stress. Previous similar hospital studies – based on all similar hospitals in the population - have shown that some work stress may be tolerated without any harm done. Based on credible prior information, it is estimated that the probability of a nurse experiencing harmful work stress is 0.105. Before the hospital decides to change the working conditions (perhaps a costly proposition) it asks all nurses to take a screening, questionnaire-type, stress test constructed in such a way so that it determines whether or not a nurse feels stressful due to work-related or due to non-work-related conditions. If the screening test generates a posterior probability greater than the prior probability, the hospital, subject to profit constraints, may decide in favor of making working conditions less conducive to work stress. On the contrary, if the posterior probability is less than the prior, the hospital may decide in favor of a more stressful environment.

Let the imaginary screening test results, or posterior information, be summarized in the cells of Figure 10 (the information in the cells is self-explanatory but some cells are identified by letters.) Listed below the matrix, in Figure 10, are:

Odds [e.g., if P_A = probability of event A, P_B = probability of event B and $P_A + P_B = 1$, the Odds in favor of event A are (P_A / P_B)];

Sensitivity (which measures how well the screening test identifies those with work stress);

Specificity (which measures how well the screening test excludes those who do not feel work stress);

Additional measures based on the above concepts.

Hence, because the posterior probability of a nurse experiencing work stress above a certain moderate level is 0.073, less than the prior probability, the hospital, subject to profit constraints, may choose to do nothing or, perhaps, establish more stressful working conditions.

Naturally, one may ask: why not totally eliminate stress in the work place? The answer is: because 'zero stress' may not necessarily correspond to maximum or even positive profit. The non-regulated firm should always search for the amount of stress (S^*) that maximizes profit (the one predicted by the model in section

II, Figure 2, above.) This S^* should be designated as the right level of stress referred to above as *certain moderate level* of stress.

Figure 10: Bayesian Learning

	Work stress present	Work stress absent	Total
Above moderate level of stress	20 = a	252	272
Moderate or less level of stress	85	643 = c	728
Total	105 = b	895 = d	1000

Above moderate level of stress:
Prior Probability = 0.105.
Prior Odds or Prevalence = (0.105 / 0.895) = 0.117.
Sensitivity = a/b = 0.19.
Specificity = c/d = 0.72.
Likelihood Ratio = (Sensitivity)/(1-Specificity) = 0.68.
Posterior Odds = (Prior Odds)(Likelihood Ratio) = 0.079.
Posterior Probability = (Posterior Odds)/(1+ Posterior Odds) = 0.073.

VI. Summary & Conclusion

In an attempt to capture the essence of issues associated with occupational stress, some neo-classical microeconomic theoretical concepts were proposed above along with a suggestion for a screening (Bayesian-type) test. Popular and professional press reports appear to justify the logic of our theoretical assertions. The main conclusions may be summarized as follows:

Firstly, assuming that stress is a factor of production and that the firm functions in an environment free of any regulation, a proposed model predicts that the profit maximizing stress level (S^*) is less than the stress level that maximizes output. Additionally, reduction below S^* may be achieved only if a firm's increase in cost for stress relief in the work place guarantees productivity and profit improvement in exchange for a reduction in employee health damages/costs due to stress. Moreover, assuming that a stress standard inside the firm can be identified, reallocation of stress from one group of employees to another, or from one production plant to another, may facilitate compliance with that standard and simultaneously contribute to a reduction in total damages to employees and/or to a reduction in total stress relief expenditures to the firm.

Secondly, governmental stress standard regulation may trigger unintended outcomes due to miss-estimation of that standard:

if the standard is considerably less than S*, the firm may not have the incentive to comply.

Thirdly, the implementation of a periodic screening test, based on Bayesian statistical analysis, may determine the optimal stress level that may be used by the firm and perhaps the regulatory authority for the determination of costs and penalties.

The paper does not shed any light on many remaining issues: (a) beyond a certain point, the measurement of stress in the work place may become very difficult to handle: how much of the observed stress is due to work and how much of it is due to the employee's personal life and how interdependent are the two? (b) Would it be prudent to make stress disputes subject to litigation and conventional negligence rules and regulations? (c) How should a firm minimize problems associated with asymmetries in information that may lead to hold up, adverse selection and moral hazard?

Regardless of the questions that remain unanswered, as of 2003, the following facts remain: (1) For US business, the per annum employee stress costs amount to about $10,000 with an aggregate economic impact on the whole economy of about $300 billion (Higbie); (2) For UK business, at least 13 million days a year are lost due of occupational stress, which affects one in five of all working people at a cost of about to 3.8 billion British pounds (Laurence); (3) In the UK, wisely or unwisely, the government has decided to intervene. (4) In the USA, preliminary studies by psychologists, focusing on stressful occupations, have demonstrated that occupational stress reduction efforts contribute to lower health care costs and to more productivity. I believe that more research has to be undertaken by economists, especially, in collaboration with psychologists, managers and government officials.

Endnotes

1. Stress is different than challenge. As explained by NIOSH "challenge energizes us psychologically and physically, and it motivates us to learn new skills and master our jobs. When a challenge is met, we feel relaxed and satisfied. Thus, challenge is an important ingredient for healthy and productive work."

2. In the remaining of his article Lawrance reports:

> *(t)he code will introduce a legal basis against which companies can be assessed for their efforts to reduce stress to manageable levels ...*
>
> *Under the Health and Safety at Work Act, companies can technically already be sued for causing unnecessary stress at work. But cases are difficult to prove and no prosecutions have been brought by the HSE. A spokeswoman said: "The management standards will be what we expect companies to do to manage the stress in their workplace. They will be equivalent to the Highway Code. It will make it easier for employees to bring actions and our inspectors will be able to go in and see if companies are up to the standards."*
>
> *More than 13 million days a year are lost because of stress, which affects one in five of all employees at a cost of up to 3.8 billion (British pounds), the HSE says.*

Bill Callaghan, chairman of the Health and Safety Commission, said: "We know there is considerable pressure in the modern workplace but there is a difference between the buzz people get from doing a busy and challenging job and an unreasonable pressure, which can harm health, lead to absence and additional strain on their colleagues trying to cope in an even more pressured environment. Handling (firms) a tool to help them develop good practice makes sense and the earlier the better. I know this is not going to be easy but grasping this nettle can make for a successful business and a happier workforce." ...

In pilot studies of the code, to uncover hidden problems companies including Sainsbury's and Lloyds TSB have focused on areas where sickness absence is highest, turnover of staff is increasing or productivity is falling. Staff have been asked to fill in questionnaires to rate the company against the six standards.

Claire Forty, occupational health manager at the energy company Innogy, said 700 of more than 2,000 staff had been surveyed and the pilot had revealed some groups were concerned at excessive demands and others about lack of control. "We have a lot of people who work a long way from where they live so flexible working, including working at home, is a big issue."

Ms Forty said companies had to acknowledge that the "whole person" came to to work and pressures at home could affect their performance at work. "If I say to my boss I have got to come in late this week because of children problems I am confident it would be accepted. Equally, if he says to me there is a big job on and I have to come in at 7:30am each day that would be no problem.

"Benefits of meeting the stress standards, apart from complying with the law, is reducing turnover and sickness absence and increasing productivity as well as making it a great place to work. We haven't had a claim for stress against us but it would be foolish for any employer to say they would never get one."

Elizabeth Gyngell, head of HSE's better-working environment division, said: "I am delighted such a wide range of companies … are working with us to develop standards and being so frank in helping tackle the challenges."

References

Blumenthal, James A.; Babyak M.; Wei J.; O'Connor C.; Waugh R.; Eisenstein E.; Mark D.; Sherwood A.; Woodley P.S.; Irwin R.J.; Reed G. Usefulness of psychosocial treatment of mental stress-induced myocardial ischemia in men. *The American Journal of Cardiology*, Vol. 89, Issue 2, January 15, 2002, Pp. 164-168.

Higbie, Andrea New York Times News Service – Section C4, *Sunday Telegram*, Worcester Massachusetts, 3/18/01.

Kantarelis, D.; Asadoorian, M. *Essentials of Inferential Statistics*, 4th Ed., University Press of America. 2004.

Laurance, Jeremy. Firms that ignore stress risks face legal action. *The Independent*, London, June 16, 2003.

National Institute for Occupational Safety and Health (NIOSH) <http://www.cdc.gov/niosh/stresswk.html> 2002.

Revicki, D.A.; Whitley, T.W. Organizational characteristics, perceived work stress, and depression in emergency medicine residents. *Hospital Topics*, Winter 1997, Vol. 75, Issue 1, pp. 30-38.

Stress Directions <www.stressdirections.com>

Sweeney, G. M; Nicholls, K.A.; Kline, P. Factors contributing to work-related stress in occupational therapists: Results from a pilot study. *British Journal of Occupational Therapy*, August, Volume 54(8), 1991, pp. 284-288.

Index (subject and name)

A

B

C

D

E

F

G

H

I

J

K

L

M

N

O

P

R

S

T

U

V

W

Y

Z